Favorite SONGS OF ISRAEL

Compiled, Edited and Arranged
by VELVEL PASTERNAK

TARA PUBLICATIONS

ISBN 0-933676-07-7

PRINTED IN THE UNITED STATES

Dedicated to the memory of

RICHARD J. NEUMANN

my teacher, colleague and friend

His talents were dedicated to our people. Jewish music has been nobly enriched by his musical creativity.

FOREWORD

FAVORITE SONGS OF ISRAEL, like two preceding collections, ISRAEL IN SONG (1974) and GREAT SONGS OF ISRAEL (1976), is a musical overview of the people of Israel rather than a volume of currently popular Israeli songs. Included in this edition are nostalgic songs of both pre and post statehood; the music of the Sephardic, Ladino and Oriental heritage; a grouping of Z'mirot (liturgical songs sung in the home to celebrate Sabbath and the Festivals); songs of the Hassidim; rounds, dances and current "hit" songs.

All selections have been transliterated beneath the music and repeated alongside the song texts to facilitate those who are not expert in the reading of Hebrew. Due to the problem of layout not all the verses of a song have been included. Capsule translations appear under the texts to make the selections more meaningful.

The editor wishes to acknowledge with gratitude the assistance of the following: my daughter, Shira, who worked with me on the overall concept of the book and whose judgment was invaluable in the selection of the material; Dr. Samuel and Tamar Fishman who painstakingly translated many of the modern Hebrew lyrics; ACUM Ltd. Israel for obtaining copyright information and clearance; the composers, lyricists and publishers who granted permission to reprint their songs.; Elly Zomick for many valued suggestions which have been incorporated in this book.

Above all, my heartfelt thanks to Goldie, my helpmate, for giving up many social amenities while her husband once again toiled in the vineyard of Jewish music.

Velvel Pasternak
Shevat, 5745

CONTENTS

POPULAR & SECULAR

SONGS OF NURIT HIRSH

NOSTALGIC SONGS

SEPHARDIC & ORIENTAL

LADINO SONGS

HASSIDIC

Z'MIROT & LITURGY

ROUNDS

FROM THE DANCE

KEY TO TRANSLITERATION

a	....	as in c*a*r
ai	....	as in s*igh*
e	....	as in f*e*d
ë	....	as in th*ey*
i	....	as in p*i*n or m*e*
o	....	as in f*o*rm or b*o*at
u	....	as in tr*ue*
'	....	as in *i*t
ch	....	as in Ba*ch*

ALPHABETICAL INDEX

CHAI

Joyously
Ehud Manor, Avi Toledano
Shim- u a - chai a - ni od chai u - shtë ë -
nai od ni - sa - ot la - or ra - bim cho - chai ach gam pra -
mor mi - dor l' -
chai u - l' - fa - nai sha - nim ra - bot mis - for a - ni sho -
dor k' - ma - - yan më - az v' - ad o - lam a - ni sho -
ël u - mit - pa - lël tov she - lo av - da od ha - tik -
va o - vër miz - tov she - lo av - da od ha - tik -
va chai chai chai kën a - ni od chai
dal 𝄋 al ⊕ poi CODA
ze ha - shir she - sa - ba shar et - mol l' - a - ba v' - ha - yom a - ni a - ni od
CODA
chai (chai chai) chai (chai chai) chai a - ni od chai chai chai

Shimu a-chai
Ani od chai
Ush-tē ē-nai od ni-sa-ot la-or
Rabim cho-chai ach gam pra-chai
U-l'-fa-nai shanim rabot mis-for
Ani sho-ēl u-mit-pa-lēl
Tov she-lo av-da od ha-tik-va

Ovër miz-mor mi-dor l'dor
K'ma-yan më-az v'ad olam
Ani sho-ēl u-mit-pa-lēl
Tov she-lo avda od hatikva
CHORUS:
Chai chai chai
Kën ani od chai.
Ze hashir she-saba shar etmol l'aba
V'hayom ani...
Ani od chai chai chai
Am Yisraël chai
Ze hashir she-saba shar etmol l'aba
V'hayom ani...

שִׁמְעוּ אָחַי
אֲנִי עוֹד חַי
וּשְׁתֵּי עֵינַי עוֹד נִשָּׂאוֹת לָאוֹר
רַבִּים חוֹכַי אַךְ גַּם פְּרָחַי
וּלְפָנַי שָׁנִים רַבּוֹת מִסְפּוֹר
אֲנִי שׁוֹאֵל וּמִתְפַּלֵּל
טוֹב שֶׁלֹּא אָבְדָה עוֹד הַתִּקְוָה

עוֹבֵר מִזְמוֹר מִדּוֹר לְדוֹר
כְּמַעְיָן מֵאָז וְעַד עוֹלָם
אֲנִי שׁוֹאֵל וּמִתְפַּלֵּל
טוֹב שֶׁלֹּא אָבְדָה עוֹד הַתִּקְוָה

פִּזְמוֹן:
חַי חַי חַי
כֵּן אֲנִי עוֹד חַי.
זֶה הַשִּׁיר שֶׁסַּבָּא שָׁר אֶתְמוֹל לְאַבָּא
וְהַיּוֹם אֲנִי . . .
אֲנִי עוֹד חַי חַי חַי
עַם יִשְׂרָאֵל חַי
זֶה הַשִּׁיר שֶׁסַּבָּא שָׁר אֶתְמוֹל לְאַבָּא
וְהַיּוֹם אֲנִי . . .

Listen brothers! I'm still alive!
Alive, Alive, indeed I am Alive!
The people of Israel are Alive.
How wonderful that hope is never lost.

HAL'LUYA

Moderato
Shimrit Or, Kobi Oshrat
A
Ha - l' - lu - ya la - o - lam
A C♯m F♯m E
ha - l' - lu - ya ya - shi - ru ku - lam
A7 D
b' - mi - la a - chat bo - dë da ha -
A C♯m F♯m Bm7
lëv ma - lë ba - ha - mon to - da v' - ho - lëm gam hu ë - ze
E7 E7 A
o - lam nif - la ha - l' - lu - ya
A A C♯m
im ha - shir ha - l' - lu - ya
F♯m E E7 D
al yom she - më - ir ha - l' - lu - ya
D♯dim A C♯7 F♯m D
al ma she - ha - ya ya u - ma she - od

הַלְלוּיָהּ לָעוֹלָם
הַלְלוּיָהּ יָשִׁירוּ כֻּלָּם
בְּמִלָּה אַחַת בּוֹדֵדָה
הַלֵּב מָלֵא בַּהֲמוֹן תּוֹדָה
וְהוֹלֵם גַּם הוּא אֵיזֶה עוֹלָם נִפְלָא

הַלְלוּיָהּ עִם הַשִּׁיר
הַלְלוּיָהּ עַל יוֹם שֶׁמֵּאִיר
הַלְלוּיָהּ עַל מַה שֶּׁהָיָה — יָהּ
וּמַה שֶּׁעוֹד לֹא הָיָה — הַלְלוּיָהּ.

Hal'luya la-o-lam
Hal'luya ya-shi-ru ku-lam
B'mi-la achat bo-dë-da
Ha-lëv ma-lë ba-ha-mon to-da
V'ho-lëm gam hu ë-ze olam nif-la

Hal'luya im hashir
Hal'luya al yom she-më-ir
Hal'luya al ma she-ha-ya—ya
U-ma she-od lo ha-ya— Hal'luya

Sing Halleluya to the world. Sing Halleluya to a bright new day. Halleluya for that which was—and for all that will be. Halleluya!

KINOR DAVID

Allegro moderato
Avihoo Medina
Lif - në sha - nim ra - bot sham- u b' - e - retz Yis - ra - ël ko -
lot ni - gun shi - ra u - miz - mo - rim bitz - lil ko m' - yu -
chad u - vin - i - ma to - va k' - shir tzi - por za -
mir bën he - a - lim bitz - lil ko m' - yu - chad u -
vin - i - ma to - va k' - shir tzi - por za - mir bën he - a -
lim ze ki - nor Da- vid b' - yad Da- vid ha- me- lech ha -
po - rët al më - ta - rav k' - tov li - bo v'- ya - yin
l' - ët e - rev m' - la - ve hu et shi - rav rav

לִפְנֵי שָׁנִים רַבּוֹת שָׁמְעוּ בְּאֶרֶץ יִשְׂרָאֵל
קוֹלוֹת נִגּוּן שִׁירָה וּמִזְמוֹרִים
בְּצְלִיל כֹּה מְיוּחָד וּבְנְעִימָה טוֹבָה
כְּשִׁיר צִפּוֹר זָמִיר בֵּין הֶעָלִים

זֶה כִּנּוֹר דָּוִד. בְּיַד דָּוִד הַמֶּלֶךְ הַפּוֹרֵט עַל מֵיתָרָיו
כְּטוֹב לִבּוֹ בְּיַיִן לְעֵת עֶרֶב מְלַוֶּה הוּא אֶת שִׁירָיו.

לִפְנֵי שָׁנִים רַבּוֹת בְּשַׁעֲרֵי יְרוּשָׁלַיִם
נִצְּבָה נִפְעֶמֶת בַּחֲלוֹן מִיכַל
הִבִּיטָה בַּמִּשְׁעוֹל וּבְעֵינֶיהָ אוֹר
רוֹקֵד דָּוִד וּבְיָדוֹ כִּנּוֹר.

Lif-në sha-nim rabot sham-u b'e-retz Yisraël
Kolot ni-gun shi-ra u-miz-mo-rim
Bitz-lil ko m'yu-chad uv'n'i-ma tova
K'shir tzipor zamir bën he-a-lim

Ze kinor David b'yad David ha-me-lech
Ha-po-rët al më-ta-rav
K'tov li-bo v'ya-yin l'ët erev
M'la-ve hu et shi-rav.

Lif-në sha-nim ra-bot bish-a-rë Y'ru-sha-la-yim
Nitz-va nif-e-met ba-cha-lon mi-chal
Hi-bi-ta ba-mish-ol uv-ë-ne-ha or
Ro-këd David uv-ya-do ki-nor.

Many years ago a beautiful song was heard in the land of Israel. This is the harp of David which accompanied his songs when his heart was gladdened by wine.

JERUSALEM IS MINE

I am the sun Jerusalem, you are a painted sky
I am a bird Jerusalem, you have the wings to fly
You are the father of my dream, I am the gift of time
I am your child Jerusalem, Jerusalem is mine
You are the orchard in the sand, I am the fruit you bear
You are the glove that warms my hands, I am the smile you wear
You are the music of the hills, I am the words that rhyme
I am your song Jerusalem, Jerusalem is mine
You are the cradle of freedom, I am the harvest of Springtime
I am the dawn of a new day, I am tomorrow, you are forever
You are my shelter from the storm, I am your guiding light
You are a book whose leaves are torn, I am the piece you write
You are the branches of a tree, I am a clinging vine
I am a prayer Jerusalem, Jerusalem is mine
I have come home Jerusalem, Jerusalem is mine

NOLAD'TI L'SHALOM

Lyrics and Music by Uzi Hitman

Moving

Dm Gm A7 Dm
A - ni no - la - d' - ti el ha - man - gi - not v' -

Bb F Gm Dm A7 Dm Gm
el ha - shi - rim shel kol ha - m' - di - not ___ no - lad - ti la - la-shon

A7 Dm Bb F Gm Dm A7
v' - gam la - ma - kom la - m' - at le - ha - mon she-yo- sheet yad la - sha - lom ___

Dm C F D Gm E7 A Dm Gm
ah ___ a - ni no - lad - ti la - sha -

Gm Dm Gm
lom she - rak ya - gi - a ___ a - ni no - lad - ti la - sha -

A7 Dm Am D7 Gm
lom she - rak ya - vo ___ a - ni no - lad - ti la - sha - lom she - rak yo - fi - a ___

Gm 1. A7 Dm
___ a - ni ro - tze a - ni ro - tze li - yot kvar bo ___

Dm Gm 2. A7 Dm
___ a - ni no - lad - ti l' - sha - tze li - yot kvar bo

Ani nolad'ti
El ha-man-gi-not
V'el hashirim
Shel kol ham-di-not

Nolad'ti la-la-shon
V'gam la-ma-kom
Lam'at le-ha-mon
She-yo-sheet yad la-sha-lom

Ah....
Ani nolad'ti la-shalom
She-rak ya-gi-a
Ani nolad'ti la-sha-lom
She-rak ya-vo
Ani nolad'ti la-shalom
She-rak yo-fi-a
Ani ro-tze, ani ro-tze
Li-yot k'var bo!

Nolad'ti l'u-ma
V'la sha-nim al-pa-yim
Sh'mura la adama
V'la chelkat shamayim

V'hi ro-a tzo-fa
Hi-në o-le hayom
V'ha-sha-a yafa–
Zo-hi sh'at-shalom

אֲנִי נוֹלַדְתִּי
אֶל הַמַּנְגִּינוֹת
וְאֶל הַשִּׁירִים
שֶׁל כָּל הַמְּדִינוֹת.

נוֹלַדְתִּי לַלָּשׁוֹן
וְגַם לַמָּקוֹם,
לַמְּעַט, לֶהָמוֹן,
שֶׁיּוֹשִׁיט יָד לַשָּׁלוֹם.

אֲהָהָ . . .
אֲנִי נוֹלַדְתִּי לַשָּׁלוֹם
שֶׁרַק יַגִּיעַ.
אֲנִי נוֹלַדְתִּי לַשָּׁלוֹם
שֶׁרַק יָבוֹא.
אֲנִי נוֹלַדְתִּי לַשָּׁלוֹם
שֶׁרַק יוֹפִיעַ
אֲנִי רוֹצֶה, אֲנִי רוֹצֶה
לִהְיוֹת כְּבָר בּוֹ!

נוֹלַדְתִּי לְאֻמָּה
וְלָהּ שָׁנִים אַלְפַּיִם
שְׁמוּרָה לָהּ אֲדָמָה
וְלָהּ חֶלְקַת שָׁמַיִם.

וְהִיא רוֹאָה, צוֹפָה:
הִנֵּה עוֹלֶה הַיּוֹם
וְהַשָּׁעָה יָפָה —
זוֹהִי שְׁעַת־שָׁלוֹם.

I was born to the themes and the songs of all countries.
I was born to the language and also to the place, to the few and to the many and will stretch out a hand to peace.

ADON OLAM

Music by Uzi Hitman

Adon olam asher malach
B'terem kol y'tzir nivra
L'ët na-a-sa b'chef-tzo kol
Azai me-lech sh'mo nik-ra

V'a-cha-rë kich-lot ha-kol
L'va-do yim-loch no-ra
V'hu haya v'hu ho-ve
V'hu yi-ye b'tif-a-ra

אֲדוֹן עוֹלָם אֲשֶׁר מָלַךְ
בְּטֶרֶם כָּל יְצִיר נִבְרָא
לְעֵת נַעֲשָׂה בְחֶפְצוֹ כֹּל
אֲזַי מֶלֶךְ שְׁמוֹ נִקְרָא.

וְאַחֲרֵי כִּכְלוֹת הַכֹּל
לְבַדּוֹ יִמְלֹךְ נוֹרָא
וְהוּא הָיָה וְהוּא הֹוֶה
וְהוּא יִהְיֶה בְּתִפְאָרָה.

He is the eternal Lord who reigned before any being was created. At the time when all was made by his will, he was at once acknowledged as King. And at the end, when all shall cease to be, the revered God alone shall still be King. He was, he is and he shall be in glorious eternity.

SHIRI LI KINNERET

Sham ha-rë go-lan ba-o-fek
Ni-tzavim od bid-ma-ma
Un-arim b'ho-lam do-fek
Od shom-rim al ha-ra-ma
Uv-yash-vam im erev saviv lam-du-ra
Onim hëm lach ki-ne-ret b'shi-ra
Shiri li kineret, shir mizmor ya-shan
Shiri li kineret, shir li ha-go-lan

Ha-du-git o-de-na sha-ta
Mif-ra-sa mal-bin ba-chof
V'chur-shat ha-ë-ka-lip-tus
Od sho-me-ret al ha-nof
Ët nif-re-set re-shet im shoch has'a-ra
Onim hëm lach kineret b'shira
Shiri li kineret...

שָׁם הָרֵי גּוֹלָן בָּאֹפֶק
נִצָּבִים עוֹד בִּדְמָמָה
וּנְעָרִים בְּהֹלָם דֹּפֶק
עוֹד שׁוֹמְרִים עַל הָרָמָה
וּבְיָשְׁבָם עִם עֶרֶב סָבִיב לַמְּדוּרָה
עוֹנִים הֵם לָךְ כִּנֶּרֶת בְּשִׁירָה
שִׁירִי לִי כִּנֶּרֶת, שִׁיר מִזְמוֹר יָשָׁן
שִׁירִי לִי כִּנֶּרֶת, שִׁיר לִי הַגּוֹלָן

הַדּוּגִית עוֹדֶנָּה שָׁטָה
מִפְרָשָׂהּ מַלְבִּין בַּחוֹף
וְחֻרְשַׁת הָאֶקָלִיפְּטוּס
עוֹד שׁוֹמֶרֶת עַל הַנּוֹף
עֵת נִפְרֶשֶׂת רֶשֶׁת עִם שַׁךְ הַסְּעָרָה
עוֹנִים הֵם לָךְ כִּנֶּרֶת בְּשִׁירָה
שִׁירִי לִי כִּנֶּרֶת . . .

The mountains of Golan still stand in silence and young men guard the heights. As they sit around the evening campfire they answer you Kinneret in song. Sing to me Kinneret, sing to me Golan.

LANER V'LIVSAMIM

Music: Avihoo Medina

לַנֵּר וְלִבְשָׂמִים נַפְשִׁי מְיַחֲלָה
אִם תִּתְּנוּ לִי כּוֹס יַיִן לְהַבְדָּלָה

Laner v'liv-sa-mim nafshi m'ya-chë-la
Im tit-nu li kos yayin l'hav-da-la

My soul awaits the candle and the incense. If you should but give me a goblet of wine for Havdala.

HAL'LUYA

Yakov Galpaz, Emanuel Gal

Adam cho-zër uk'tzir yo-mo
Tza-nu-a hu va-dal
V'al ga-bo tza-rot ha-chol
Om-sot lo k'mig-dal.
Hu l'fa-nav ro-e pit-om
Et sh'te ë-ne-ha shel bi-to
V'hu az shar v'hën i-to
Sha-rot Hal'luya

Hal'luya v'ze hashir
O-le mikol pi-not ha-ir,
K'she-ha-adam ush'të ë-në bi-to
Sharim Hal'luya.

אָדָם חוֹזֵר וּקְצִיר יוֹמוֹ
צָנוּעַ הוּא וָדַל.
וְעַל גַּבּוֹ צָרוֹת הַחוֹל
עוֹמְסוֹת לוֹ כְּמִגְדָּל.
הוּא לְפָנָיו רוֹאֶה פִּתְאוֹם
אֶת שְׁתֵּי עֵינֶיהָ שֶׁל בִּתּוֹ
וְהוּא אָז שָׁר וְהֵן אִתּוֹ
שָׁרוֹת הַלְלוּיָהּ.

הַלְלוּיָהּ וְזֶה הַשִּׁיר
עוֹלֶה מִכָּל פִּנּוֹת הָעִיר,
כְּשֶׁהָאָדָם וּשְׁתֵּי עֵינֵי בִּתּוֹ
שָׁרִים הַלְלוּיָהּ.

A man returns from a modest and meager day, bearing the weight of ordinary troubles. Suddenly he sees his daughter's eyes and sings with them Haleluya. Haleluya, this is the song arising from all over the town, when a man and his daughter's eyes sing Haleluya.

ERETZ YISRAEL YAFA

נַעֲרָה טוֹבָה יְפַת עֵינַיִם
לָנוּ יֵשׁ בְּאֶרֶץ יִשְׂרָאֵל,
וְ״יֶלֶד טוֹב יְרוּשָׁלַיִם״
הוֹ מִי פִּלֵּל וּמִי מִלֵּל.

וְתוֹרָה־אוֹרָה כָּזוֹ יֵשׁ לָנוּ
וְגַם הַגָּדָה וּמְגִלָּה,
וֵאלֹהִים אֶחָד שֶׁלָּנוּ,
וְקוֹל חָתָן וְקוֹל כַּלָּה.

פִּזְמוֹן:
אֶרֶץ יִשְׂרָאֵל יָפָה,
אֶרֶץ יִשְׂרָאֵל פּוֹרַחַת
אַתְּ יוֹשְׁבָה בָּהּ וְצוֹפָה
אַתְּ צוֹפָה בָּהּ וְזוֹרַחַת.

Na-a-ra tova y'fat ë-na-yim
La-nu yësh b'e-retz Yisraël
V'ye-led tov Y'ru-sha-la-yim
Ho mi pi-lrl u-mi mi-lël

V'-to-ra-ora ka-zo yësh lanu
V'gam Ha-ga-da u-m'gila
Vë-lo-him e-chad she-la-nu
V'kol cha-tan v'kol ka-la.

Chorus:
Eretz Yisrael ya-fa,
Eretz Yisrael po-ra-chat
At yosh-va ba v'tzo-fa
At tzo-fa ba v'zo-ra-chat.

We have a good girl, fair-eyed,
In the Land of Israel
And a good boy, Jerusalem
Who would have thought so
Or said it?
We have the light of Torah
And Haggadah and Megilla.
We have one God
And the voice of bridegroom and bride.

Beautiful Land of Israel
Flowering Land of Israel
You dwell there and look forth
You look forth and shine.

ERETZ, ERETZ

Moderato
Lyrics and Music by Y. Paikov
Em Em/D C C/A
E - retz e - retz e - retz e - retz tchol ën av v' - ha-she -
B B7 Em B B7 Em Em/D
mesh la kid - vash v' - cha - lav e - retz ba no - lad - nu
C C/A B B7 Em
e - retz ba nich - ye v' - në-shëv ba yi - ye ma she - yi -ye
Am Em Am Em C G
e - retz she - no - hav hi la - nu ëm va - av e - retz shel ha - am
C G C G
e - retz l' - o - lam e - retz ba no-lad - nu e -
Am Em Ebdim B7 Em
- retz ba nich - ye yi - ye ma she - yi - ye

Eretz, eretz, eretz,
Eretz tchol ën av,
V'ha-she-mesh la kid-vash v'cha-lav
Eretz ba no-lad-nu
Eretz ba nich-ye,
V'në-shëv ba, yi-ye ma she-yi-ye.

Eretz she-no-hav
Hi lanu ëm va-av
Eretz shel ha-am
Eretz l'olam
Eretz ba nolad-nu eretz ba nich-ye
Yi-ye ma she-yi-ye.

Eretz, eretz, eretz,
Yam el mul ha-chof,
Uf-ra-chim vi-la-dim bli sof.
Ba-tza-fon ki-ne-ret
Ba-tza-fon ki-ne-ret
Ba-da-rom cho-lot,
U-mi-miz-rach l'ma-a-rav no-shëk gvu-lot.

Eretz she-no-hav...

אֶרֶץ, אֶרֶץ, אֶרֶץ,
אֶרֶץ תְּכוֹל אֵין עָב,
וְהַשֶּׁמֶשׁ לָהּ כִּדְבַשׁ וְחָלָב.
אֶרֶץ בָּהּ נוֹלַדְנוּ
אֶרֶץ בָּהּ נִחְיֶה,
וְנֵשֵׁב בָּהּ, יִהְיֶה מַה שֶּׁיִּהְיֶה.

אֶרֶץ שֶׁנֹּאהַב
הִיא לָנוּ אֵם וָאָב
אֶרֶץ שֶׁל הָעָם
אֶרֶץ לְעוֹלָם
אֶרֶץ בָּהּ נוֹלַדְנוּ אֶרֶץ בָּהּ נִחְיֶה
יִהְיֶה מַה שֶּׁיִּהְיֶה.

אֶרֶץ, אֶרֶץ, אֶרֶץ,
יָם אֶל מוּל הַחוֹף,
וּפְרָחִים וִילָדִים בְּלִי סוֹף.
בַּצָּפוֹן כִּנֶּרֶת
בַּדָּרוֹם חוֹלוֹת,
וּמִמִּזְרָח לְמַעֲרָב נוֹשֵׁק גְּבוּלוֹת.

אֶרֶץ שֶׁנֹּאהַב . . .

O blue and cloudless land
For her the sun is like milk and honey.
A land in which we were born,
A land in which we shall live
And in which we shall dwell —
Whatever will be will be.
A land which we love is mother and father to us.
A land of the people, a land forever,
A land in which we were born
A land in which we shall live
Whatever will be will be.

CHAG YOVEL

Or ya-rad al ha-ga-lil
Mit-mo-gëg lo ha-kar-mel
Ha-gil-bo-a shar b'gil
Shar gam ëmek yiz-r'ël

Baki-ne-ret tzo-ho-la
Ha-yar-dën sho-tëf ba-hir
M'ra-ke-det hash-fë-la
Vi-ru-sha-la-yim shir.

Chag, chag, chag yo-vël
al kol eretz Yis-ra-ël
Al kol eretz Yis-ra-ël
Chag yo-vël.

אוֹר יָרַד עַל הַגָּלִיל
מִתְמוֹגֵג לוֹ הַכַּרְמֶל
הַגִּלְבֹּעַ שָׁר בְּגִיל
שָׁר גַּם עֵמֶק יִזְרְעֵאל.

בַּכִּנֶּרֶת צָהֳלָה
הַיַּרְדֵּן שׁוֹטֵף בָּהִיר
מְרַקֶּדֶת הַשְּׁפֵלָה
וִירוּשָׁלַיִם שִׁיר.

פִּזְמוֹן:
חַג, חַג, חַג יוֹבֵל
עַל כָּל אֶרֶץ יִשְׂרָאֵל
עַל כָּל אֶרֶץ יִשְׂרָאֵל
חַג יוֹבֵל.

Light descends on the Galilee, the Carmel feels such pleasure. Mt. Gilboa and the Valley of Jezreel sing for joy. Celebration, celebration, for all of Israel there is a celebration.

SIM SHALOM

שִׂים שָׁלוֹם טוֹבָה וּבְרָכָה, חֵן וָחֶסֶד וְרַחֲמִים
עָלֵינוּ וְעַל כָּל יִשְׂרָאֵל עַמֶּךָ.

Sim shalom tova uv-racha, chën va-che-sed vra-cha-mim
a-lë-nu v'al kol Yisraël a-me-cha.

O grant peace, happiness, blessing, grace, kindness and mercy to us and to all Israel your people.

MALACH MISULAM YAAKOV

Y. Tahar-Lev, N. Hirsh

In the morning a white-winged angel descended from heaven on Jacob's ladder, to the dewy lawn of my house. Where do you come from and where are you going? From the Negev to Gilead. Who will you see there, our good angel? The tent of Esau and the house of Jacob.

בַּבֹּקֶר אֶל דֶּשֶׁא בֵּיתִי הָרָטֹב
אֶל דֶּשֶׁא בֵּיתִי הָרָטֹב
יָרַד מִשָּׁמַיִם בְּלֹבֶן כְּנָפַיִם
מַלְאָךְ מִסֻּלַּם יַעֲקֹב.

מֵאַיִן תָּבוֹאָה וְאָנָה תִּצְעַד?
מֵאֶרֶץ הַנֶּגֶב אֶל אֶרֶץ גִּלְעָד.
אֶת מִי שָׁם תִּרְאֶה מַלְאָכֵנוּ הַטּוֹב?
אֶת אֹהֶל עֵשָׂו וְאֶת בֵּית יַעֲקֹב.

בְּטֶרֶם אֶפְתַּח אֶת דַּלְתִּי לִקְרָאתוֹ
אֶפְתַּח אֶת דַּלְתִּי לִקְרָאתוֹ
פָּרַשׂ הַכְּנָפַיִם וְעָף לַשָּׁמַיִם
מַלְאָךְ מִסֻּלַּם יַעֲקֹב.

Ba-bo-ker el de-she bë-ti ha-ra-tov
El de-she bë-ti ha-ra-tov
Ya-rad mi-sha-ma-yim b'lo-ven k'na-fa-yim
Mal-ach mi-su-lam Ya-a-kov.

Më-ayin ta-vo-a v'a-na titz-ad
Më-eretz ha-ne-gev el eretz gil-ad
Et mi sham tir-e mal-a-chënu hatov
Et o-hel ë-sav v'et bët ya-a-kov

B'terem ef-tach et dal-ti lik-ra-to
Ef-tach et dal-ti lik-ra-to
Pa-ras hak-na-fayim v'af la-sha-mayim
Mal-ach mi-su-lam Ya-a-kov

MAKHELA ALIZA

Lea Naor, Nurit Hirsh

על רֹאשׁ הַבְּרוֹשׁ שֶׁבֶּחָצֵר
שִׂמְחָה וַהֲמֻלָּה,
שָׁם כָּל הַצִּפֳּרִים בָּעִיר
הֵקִימוּ מַקְהֵלָה

הָעֶפְרוֹנִית הַסּוֹלָנִית
נִקְּתָה אֶת הַגָּרוֹן
שִׁלְּבָה כָּנָף,
זָקְפָה מַקּוֹר
וְגַם פָּצְחָה בְּרֹן.

צִיף צִיף, שְׁרִיק שְׁרַק
בּוּל בּוּל בּוּל בּוּל בִּיל בַּל
לַה לַה לַה . . .
וְכָל מִי שֶׁשָּׁמַע אָמַר,
אַח, אֵיזוֹ מַקְהֵלָה.

פִּתְאוֹם הִפְסִיק אֶת הַשִּׁירָה
פָּשׁוֹשׁ אֶחָד זָעִיר
אִם אֵין מִלִּים וְאֵין תָּוִים
הוּא לֹא מוּכָן לָשִׁיר

אֲנַחְנוּ לֹא רוֹצִים מִלִּים
רָגְזוּ הַבֻּלְבּוּלִים
אֲנַחְנוּ גַּם לְלֹא מִלִּים
נוֹרָא מִתְבַּלְבְּלִים

צִיף צִיף, שְׁרִיק שְׁרַק . . .

Al rosh hab-rosh she-be-cha-tzër
Sim-cha va-ha-mu-la
Sham kol ha-tzi-po-rim ba-ir
Hë-ki-mu mak-hë-la

Ha-ef-ro-nit ha-so-la-nit
Nik-ta et ha-ga-ron
Shil-va ka-naf,
Zak-fa ma-kor
V'gam patz-cha b'ron.

Tzif tzif, shrik shrak
Bul bul bul bul bil bal
La la la ...
V'chol mi she-sha-ma amar,
Ach, ë-zo mak-hë-la.

Pitom hif-sik et ha-shi-ra
Pashosh echad za-ir
Im ën mi-lim v'ën ta-vim
Hu lo mu-chan la-shir

Anachnu lo ro-tzim mi-lim
Rag-zu ha-bil-bu-lim
A-nach-nu gam l'lo milim
No-ra mit-bal-ba-lim

Tzif tzif, shrik shrak ...

Atop the cypress in the courtyard, joy and shouting;
all the birds in town have joined in choir!

EL HADERECH

Once again, let's go out to the road,
Hand in hand, a golden chain.
Once again, let's go out to the road,
One people, carrying our song.
To the gates of heaven we shall certainly come,
In a while, if not now.
To the gates of heaven we shall certainly come—
For our song is not in vain.

וְשׁוּב נֵצֵאָה אֶל הַדֶּרֶךְ
יָד בְּיָד לַדֶּרֶךְ
בְּשַׁלְשֶׁלֶת זָהָב.
וְשׁוּב נֵצֵאָה אֶל הַדֶּרֶךְ
עַם אֶחָד לַדֶּרֶךְ
וְשִׁירֵנוּ עַל גַּב.

וְעַד לְשַׁעֲרֵי רָקִיעַ
בְּוַדַּאי נַגִּיעַ
עוֹד מְעַט
אִם לֹא עַכְשָׁו.
וְעַד לְשַׁעֲרֵי רָקִיעַ
בְּוַדַּאי נַגִּיעַ —
כִּי דַּרְכֵּנוּ לֹא לַשָּׁוְא.

V'shuv në-tzë-a el ha-de-rech
Yad b'yad la-de-rech
B'shal-she-let za-hav
V'shuv në-tzë-a el ha-de-rech
Am echad la-de-rech
V'shi-rë-nu al gav
V'ad l'sha-a-rë ra-ki-a
B'va-dai na-gi-a
Od m'at
Im lo achshav
V'ad l'sha-a-rë ra-ki-a
B'va-dai na-gi-a
Ki dar-kë-nu lo la-shav

HAMISHPACHA SHELI

Yoram Tahar-Lev, Nurit Hirsh

Ze hit-chil mi-shnë horim
A-li-zim utz-i-rim
She-ho-li-du bish-vi-li
Et ha-mish-pa-cha she-li
Uch-she-yësh li m'si-ba
Rak ta-bi-tu mi she-ba:

Saba ba
Aba ba
Aryë mikfar saba ba
Ba baruch
Baruch ha-ba
Im do-da– do-da - raba!
Saba ba
Aba ba
Gam ha-sav-ta ya ba ba
A-ha-lan u-mar-cha-ba
Mi she-ba baruch ha-ba!

Me-vi-im li ma-ta-not
Gam g'do-lot v'gam k'ta-not
Ma-ni-chim hëm ba-pi-na
V'yotz-im el ha-gi-na
M'nash-kim et a-cho-ti
U-va-im litz-bot o-ti

Saba ba...

זֶה הִתְחִיל מִשְּׁנֵי הוֹרִים
עַלִּיזִים וּצְעִירִים
שֶׁהוֹלִידוּ בִּשְׁבִילִי
אֶת הַמִּשְׁפָּחָה שֶׁלִּי
וּכְשֶׁיֵּשׁ לִי מְסִבָּה
רַק תַּבִּיטוּ מִי שֶׁבָּא:

סַבָּא בָּא
אַבָּא בָּא
אַרְיֵה מִכְּפַר־סַבָּא בָּא
בָּא בָּרוּךְ
בָּרוּךְ הַבָּא
עִם דוֹדָה — דוֹדָה־רַבָּה!
סַבָּא בָּא
אַבָּא בָּא
גַּם הַסַּבְתָּא יַה בַּה בַּה
אַהֲלָן וּמַרְחַבָּא
מִי שֶׁבָּא בָּרוּךְ הַבָּא!

מְבִיאִים לִי מַתָּנוֹת
גַּם גְּדוֹלוֹת וְגַם קְטַנּוֹת
מַנִּיחִים הֵם בַּפִּנָּה
וְיוֹצְאִים אֶל הַגִּנָּה
מְנַשְּׁקִים אֶת אֲחוֹתִי
וּבָאִים לִצְבֹּט אוֹתִי

סַבָּא בָּא . . .

It all began with my two young parents who started our family.
And when there is a party everybody comes. All are most welcome.

PERACH HALILACH

Uri Asaf, Nurit Hirsh

Today, perhaps, we'll put off the coming of night, and not strive for the light of a star. You and I have all that we ask. We know without words that we love.

הַיּוֹם, אוּלַי, נִדְחֶה אֶת בּוֹא הַלַּיְלָה
וְלֹא נִשְׁאַף לְאוֹר כּוֹכָב
הֵן לִי וְלָךְ יֵשׁ כָּל אֲשֶׁר נִשְׁאָלָה
מִבְּלִי מִלִּים נֵדַע זֹאת כִּי נֹאהַב.

שׁוֹתְקִים נֹאהַב, כִּי לִי וְלָךְ
דַּי בְּלִי מִלִּים, שֶׁהֵן לְאֵלֶּה
אֲשֶׁר אֵינָם יוֹדְעִים לוֹמַר אַחֶרֶת
כַּמָּה יָפֶה פּוֹרֵחַ הַלִּילָךְ.

הַיּוֹם, אוּלַי, נִדְחֶה אֶת קֵץ דַּרְכֵּנוּ
וְלֹא נִזְכֹּר כִּי סוֹף לַכֹּל
זֶה הַמִּשְׁעוֹל שֶׁבּוֹ דּוֹרְכוֹת רַגְלֵינוּ
בִּשְׁנֵי קְצוֹתָיו הָעֵשֶׂב לֹא יִבֹּל.

שׁוֹתְקִים נֹאהַב, כִּי לִי וְלָךְ . . .

Hayom u-lai nid-che et bo ha-lai-la
V'lo nish-af l'or ko-chav
Hĕn li v'lach yĕsh kol asher nish-a-la
Mib-li mi-lim nĕ-da zot ki no-hav

Shot-kim no-hav, ki li v'lach
Dai b'li mi-lim, she-hĕn l'ĕ-le
Asher ĕ-nam yod-im lo-mar a-che-ret
Ka-ma ya-fe po-rĕ-ach ha-li-lach

Hayom u-lai nid-che et kĕtz dar-kĕ-nu
V'lo niz-kor ki sof la-kol
Ze ha-mish-ol she-bo dor-chot rag-lĕ-nu
Bish-nĕ k'tzo-tav ha-ĕ-sev lo yi-bol

Shot-kim no-hav ki li v'lach...

BO B'SHALOM

Rachel Shapira, Nurit Hirsh

צִפֳּרֵי הַצָּפוֹן כְּבָר הִגִּיעוּ
מִתְעַרְבֵּל הָאָבָק בַּגְּבָעוֹת
אֲחוֹתֵנוּ הָרוּחַ עָבְרָה בַּדְּרָכִים
וַאֲנַחְנוּ צְמֵאִים לְאוֹת.

בּוֹא בְּשָׁלוֹם, נִפְתָּחוֹת חֲצֵרוֹת
עָרַכְנוּ שֻׁלְחָן וְהִדְלַקְנוּ נֵרוֹת
וּבְטֶרֶם יוּשַׁר מִזְמוֹר
נְחַכֶּה לָךְ שֶׁתַּחֲזוֹר.

בּוֹא בְּשָׁלוֹם, הַחֻרְשָׁה מַזְכִּירָה
בְּטֶרֶם חֶלְקָה אַחֲרוֹנָה תִּזָּרַע
וּבְטֶרֶם יוּגַף חַלּוֹן
אָנָּא, שׁוּב אֵלֵינוּ בְּשָׁלוֹם.
מִתְרַפֵּק הָאֵזוֹב עַל הָאֶבֶן
כְּתִינוֹק עַל אִמּוֹ הַיְחִידָה
אֲחוֹתֵנוּ הָרוּחַ עָבְרָה בַּשָּׂדוֹת
וְהַגֶּשֶׁם בְּכַף־יָדָהּ.

בּוֹא בְּשָׁלוֹם, הַחֻרְשָׁה מַזְכִּירָה . . .

Tzi-po-rë ha-tza-fon kvar hi-gi-u
Mit-ar-bël ha-a-vak bag-va-ot
A-cho-të-nu ha-ru-ach av-ra bad-ra-chim
Va-a-nach-nu tz'më-im l'ot.

Bo b'shalom, nif-ta-chot cha-tzë-rot
A-rach-nu shul-chan v'hid-lak-nu në-rot
Uv-te-rem yu-shar miz-mor
N'cha-ke lach she-ta-cha-zor.

Bo b'sha-lom, ha-chor-sha maz-ki-ra
B'te-rem chel-ka a-cha-ro-na ti-za-ra
Uv-te-rem yu-gaf cha-lon
Ana, shuv ë-lë-nu b'shalom
Mit-ra-pëk ha-ë-zov al ha-e-ven
K'ti-nok al i-mo ha-y'-chi-da
A-cho-të-nu ha-ru-ach av-ra ba-sa-dot
V'ha-ge-shem b'chaf-yada

Bo b'shalom ha-chor-sha maz-ki-ra...

The birds of the North have arrived,
The dust of the hills is astir,
Our sister, the wind, has passed by the way,
And we thirst for a sign.
Come in peace, the grove reminisces,
Before the last plot is sown,
And before the window is closed, we ask,
Return to us in peace.

AL CHOMOTAYICH Y'RUSHALAYIM

עַל חוֹמוֹתַיִךְ יְרוּשָׁלַיִם הִפְקַדְתִּי שׁוֹמְרִים כָּל הַיּוֹם וְכָל הַלַּיְלָה.

Al cho-mo-ta-yich Y'rushalayim hif-ka-d'ti shomrim
Kol hayom v'chol ha-lai-la

I have set watchmen upon thy walls O, Jerusalem. They shall never hold their peace, day or night.

SASON VIKAR

Megilat Esther
Music: Nurit Hirsh

U-mor-d'-chai ya-tza mi-lif-në ha-me-lech
Bil-vush mal-chut va-a-te-ret za-hav
U-mor-d'-chai ya-tza mi-lif-në ha-me-lech
V'ha-ir shu-shshan tzo-ho-la v'sa-më-cha

La-y'hu-dim hai-ta
Ora v'simcha
Ora v'simcha
V'sa-son vi-kar

וּמָרְדְּכַי יָצָא מִלִּפְנֵי הַמֶּלֶךְ
בִּלְבוּשׁ מַלְכוּת וַעֲטֶרֶת זָהָב
וּמָרְדְּכַי יָצָא מִלִּפְנֵי הַמֶּלֶךְ
וְהָעִיר שׁוּשָׁן צָהֲלָה וְשָׂמֵחָה.

לַיְּהוּדִים הָיְתָה
אוֹרָה וְשִׂמְחָה
אוֹרָה וְשִׂמְחָה
וְשָׂשׂוֹן וִיקָר.

And Mordecai went out from the presence of the king in royal apparel and a crown of gold. And the city of Shushan shouted and was glad. The Jews had light and gladness, joy and honor.

OR VIRUSHALAYIM

הַשֶּׁקֶט שׁוּב צוֹנֵחַ כָּאן בִּשְׁמֵי־הָעֶרֶב
כְּדְאִיַּת דַּיָּה מֵעַל הַתְּהוֹמוֹת
וְשֶׁמֶשׁ אֲדֻמָּה נוֹשֶׁקֶת לַהַט חֶרֶב
אֶת הַפְּסָגוֹת הַמִּגְדָּלִים וְהַחוֹמוֹת.

פִּזְמוֹן:
רָאִיתִי עִיר עוֹטֶפֶת אוֹר
וְהִיא עוֹלָה בִּשְׁלַל צִבְעֵי־הַקֶּשֶׁת
וְהִיא נוֹגֶנֶת בִּי כְּנֵבֶל הֶעָשׂוֹר
רָאִיתִי עִיר עוֹטֶפֶת אוֹר.
הִנֵּה זוֹחֵל הַצֵּל מִבֵּין גִּבְעוֹת־הָאֹרֶן
קָרֵב בַּסֵּתֶר כְּאוֹהֵב אֶל הַשְּׁכוּנוֹת.
וּמוּל פָּנָיו קְרִיצוֹת, רִבּוֹא עֵינֵי הָאוֹר הֵן
לְפֶתַע נִפְקְחוּ אֵלַי כְּנִפְעָמוֹת.

Ha-she-ket shuv tzo-në-ach kan bish-më ha-erev
Ki-d'-i-yat da-ya më-al ha-t'ho-mot
V'shemesh a-du-ma no-she-ket la-hat che-rev
Et hap-sa-got ha-mig-da-lim v'ha-cho-mot

Ra-i-ti ir o-te-fet or
V'hi o-la bish-lal tziv-ë—ha-ke-shet
V'hi no-ge-net bi k'në-vel he-a-sor
Ra-i-ti ir o-te-fet or
Hi-në zo-chël ha-tzël mi-bën giv-ot ha-oren
Ka-rëv ba-së-ter k'o-hëv el hash-chu-not
U-mul pa-nav k'ri-tzot, ri-bo ë-në ha-or hën
L'fe-ta nif-k'chu ë-lai k'nif-a-mot

Silence again descends in the evening sky like a kite gliding above the deep. The red sun kisses the blazing sword, the peaks, the towers, the walls. I saw a city wrapped in light, arising in rainbow colors. It plays on me like a ten-stringed harp. I saw a city wrapped in light.

ASHRE HAGAFRUR

Hana Senesh, David Zehavi

אַשְׁרֵי הַגַּפְרוּר שֶׁנִּשְׂרַף וְהִצִּית לֶהָבוֹת.
אַשְׁרֵי הַלֶּהָבָה שֶׁבָּעֲרָה בְּסִתְרֵי לְבָבוֹת.
אַשְׁרֵי הַלְּבָבוֹת שֶׁיָּדְעוּ לַחְדֹּל בְּכָבוֹד.
אַשְׁרֵי הַגַּפְרוּר שֶׁנִּשְׂרַף וְהִצִּית לֶהָבוֹת.

Ash-rë ha-gaf-rur she-nis-raf v'hi-tzit le-ha-vot
Ash-rë ha-le-ha-va she-ba-a-ra b'sit-rë l'va-vot
Ash-rë hal-va-vot she-yad'-u lach-dol b'cha-vod
Ash-rë ha-gaf-rur she-nis-raf v'hi-tzit le-ha-vot.

Happy the match consumed kindling a flame.
Happy the flame, burning in the hidden depths of hearts.
Happy the hearts that stopped beating with pride;
Happy the match, consumed kindling a flame.

SHIR ERES NEGBI

Ru-ach, ru-ach al bë-të-nu
V'-cho-chav o-ro tzo-fën
Aba sham cho-rësh s'do-të-nu
Nu-ma, nu-ma bën.

La-ma ze ya-cha-rosh ba-lai-la
V'o-ti lo y'ya-shën?
Ad-ma-të-nu, b'ni ën p'nai la
Nu-ma, bën. nu-ma bën.

רוּחַ, רוּחַ עַל בֵּיתֵנוּ
וְכוֹכָב אוֹרוֹ צוֹפֵן
אַבָּא שָׁם חוֹרֵשׁ שְׂדוֹתֵינוּ
נוּמָה, נוּמָה בֵּן.

לָמָּה זֶה יַחֲרֹשׁ בַּלַּיְלָה
וְאוֹתִי לֹא יְיַשֵּׁן?
אַדְמָתֵנוּ, בְּנִי, אֵין פְּנַאי לָהּ,
נוּמָה, בֵּן. נוּמָה, בֵּן.

Out there the wind blows and the stars shine. Father plows our field. Why must he plow at night. The land is ours son—there is no time.

EFO HABACHUROT

Yosi Gamzu

K'she-bag-rush ha-ya chor v'ho-tzë-nu
Et haz-man al bi-tzot uch-vi-shim
Lo ha-yu cha-ti-chot b'ar-tzë-nu
Ach ha-yu, ya cha-bi-bi, na-shim.

Ach, ë-fo ë-fo hën
Ha-ba-chu-rot ha-hën
Im ha-ku-ku v'ha-sa-ra-fan
Im ha-tu-ri-ya v'ha-shib-ri-ya
La-ma kvar lo ro-im o-tan.

כְּשֶׁבַּגְּרוּשׁ הָיָה חוֹר וְהוֹצֵאנוּ
אֶת הַזְּמַן עַל בִּצּוֹת וּכְבִישִׁים
לֹא הָיוּ חֲתִיכוֹת בְּאַרְצֵנוּ
אַךְ הָיוּ, יָא חַבִּיבִּי, נָשִׁים.

אָח, אֵיפֹה אֵיפֹה הֵן
הַבַּחוּרוֹת הָהֵן
עִם הַקּוּקוּ וְהַסָּרָפָן
עִם הַטּוּרִיָּה וְהַשִּׁבְרִיָּה
לָמָּה כְּבָר לֹא רוֹאִים אוֹתָן.

When we first began to clear this land Israel had real women. Where are those lovlies now? Why are they no longer seen?

LIVLEVU NETZE

Liv-lu agas v'gam ta-pu-ach
Ar-pi-lim ki-su et ha-na-har
V'kat-yush-ka az tatz-a la-su-ach
E-lë chof ta-lul v'ne-dar

Në-tzë lakrav na-gën al ad-ma-tënu
Lo n'va-tër af sha-al a-da-ma
Në-tzë lak-rav na-gën al a-ti-dë-nu
Al hes-gë ar-tzënu hay'ka-ra

לִבְלְבוּ אַגָּס וְגַם תַּפּוּחַ
עַרְפִלִּים כִּסּוּ אֶת הַנָּהָר.
וְקַטְיוּשְׁקָה אָז יָצְאָה לָשׂוּחַ
אֱלֵי חוֹף תָּלוּל וְנֶהְדָּר.

נֵצֵא לַקְּרָב נָגֵן עַל אַדְמָתֵנוּ
לֹא נְוַתֵּר, אַף שַׁעַל אֲדָמָה,
נֵצֵא לַקְּרָב נָגֵן עַל עֲתִידֵנוּ
עַל הֶשֵּׂגֵי אַרְצֵנוּ הַיְקָרָה.

While the apples and pears blossom the katyushka fall. We shall fight to defend our land, our future, our precious country.

LO HARUACH

לֹא הָרוּחַ הוּא אֲשֶׁר יָצָא לוֹ
לְשׁוֹטֵט בָּעֲרָבָה.
עֲנַן אָבָק נִשָּׂא בַּדֶּרֶךְ
חֵיל פָּרָשִׁים, מֵיטַב הַחֲטִיבָה.

פִּזְמוֹן:
לֹא נְהַסֵּסָה, לָצֵאת בִּזְרוֹעַ
כָּל מִי שֶׁבָּנוּ יְנַסֶּה לִפְגּוֹעַ.
נֶשֶׁק בַּיָּדַיִם, לֹא נִטְבַּע בַּמַּיִם
לֹא נֵירָא מִבּוֹא בָּאֵשׁ.

Lo ha-ru-ach hu asher ya-tza lo
L'sho-tët ba-a-ra-va
Anan avak nisa baderech
Chël pa-ra-shim më-tav ha-cha-ti-va
Lo n'ha-së-sa la-tzët biz-ro-a
Kol mi she-ba-nu y'na-së lif-go-a
Neshek ba-ya-da-yim, lo nitba ba-mayim
Lo nira mi-bo ba-ësh

It was not the wind but a group of riders (the best of their unit) that caused the dust cloud on the road. We will not hesitate to defend ourselves against anyone who attempts to harm us.

RO-E V'RO-A

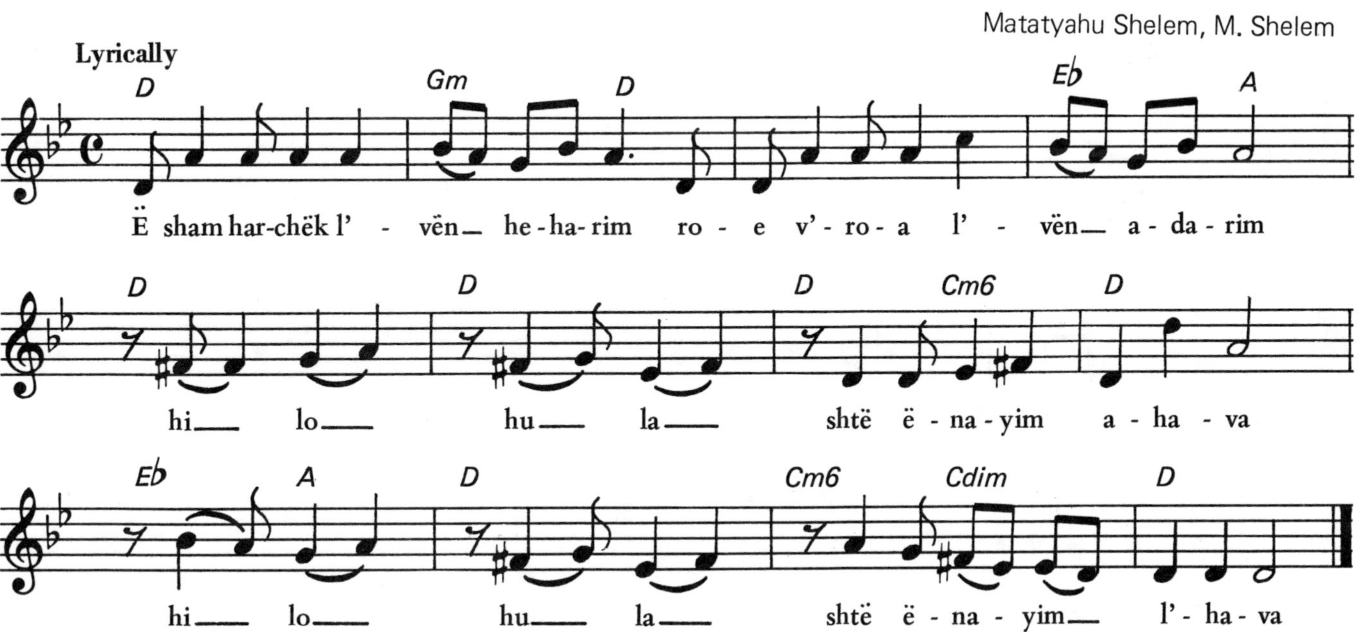

Ë-sham har-chëk bën he-ha-rim
Ro-e v'ro-a l'vën a-da-rim

Hi lo, hu la,
Shtë ë-nayim a-ha-va,
Hi lo, hu la,
Shtë ë-nayim le-ha-va.

Ë sham ba-cho-resh l'vën ha-si-chim
Ro-e v'ro-a bë-nam m'si-chim.

Hi lo...

אֵי־שָׁם הַרְחֵק בֵּין הֶהָרִים
רוֹעֶה וְרוֹעָה לְבֵין עֲדָרִים.

הִיא לוֹ, הוּא לָהּ,
שְׁתֵּי עֵינַיִם אַהֲבָה,
הִיא לוֹ, הוּא לָהּ
שְׁתֵּי עֵינַיִם לֶהָבָה.

אֵי שָׁם בַּחֹרֶשׁ לְבֵין הַשִּׂיחִים
רוֹעֶה וְרוֹעָה בֵּינָם מְשִׂיחִים.

הִיא לוֹ . . .

An idyllic love scene of a shepherd and shepherdess in the Judean hills. "He is hers; she is his."

AL TIRA AVDI YAAKOV

Al tira, avdi Ya-a-kov
Hoy cha-lam-ti cha-lom,
Al tira, avdi Ya-a-kov,
Ma no-ra ha-ma-kom!
Ni-tzav lo ha-su-lam
Im mal-a-chë sha-ma-yim
Yordim v'olim ku-lam
Im tz'cho-rë ch'na-fa-yim
Yi-shar ko-cha-cha, Ya-a-kov a-cha!
Ku-ma l'dar-k'cha këd-ma, miz-ra-cha
Lëch kadima, al ta-chat, lëch l'cha,
Ki ta-kum ha-a-retz a-ta, l'cha ul'zar-a-cha!

אַל תִּירָא, עַבְדִּי יַעֲקֹב,
הוֹי, חָלַמְתִּי, חָלוֹם,
אַל תִּירָא, עַבְדִּי יַעֲקֹב,
מַה נּוֹרָא הַמָּקוֹם!
נִצָּב לוֹ הַסֻּלָּם
עִם מַלְאֲכֵי שָׁמַיִם
יוֹרְדִים וְעוֹלִים כֻּלָּם
עִם צְחוֹרֵי־כְנָפַיִם . . .

יִישַׁר־כֹּחֲךָ, יַעֲקֹב אָחָא!
קוּמָה לְדַרְכְּךָ קֵדְמָה, מִזְרָחָה!
לֵךְ קָדִימָה,
אַל תַּחַת,
לֵךְ לְךָ,
כִּי תָקוּם
הָאָרֶץ עַתָּה,
לְךָ וּלְזַרְעֲךָ!

The Lord consoles Jacob. "Fear not the dream, my servant Jacob. Advance eastward, for this land will be thine and thy children's."

RUACH M'VADERET

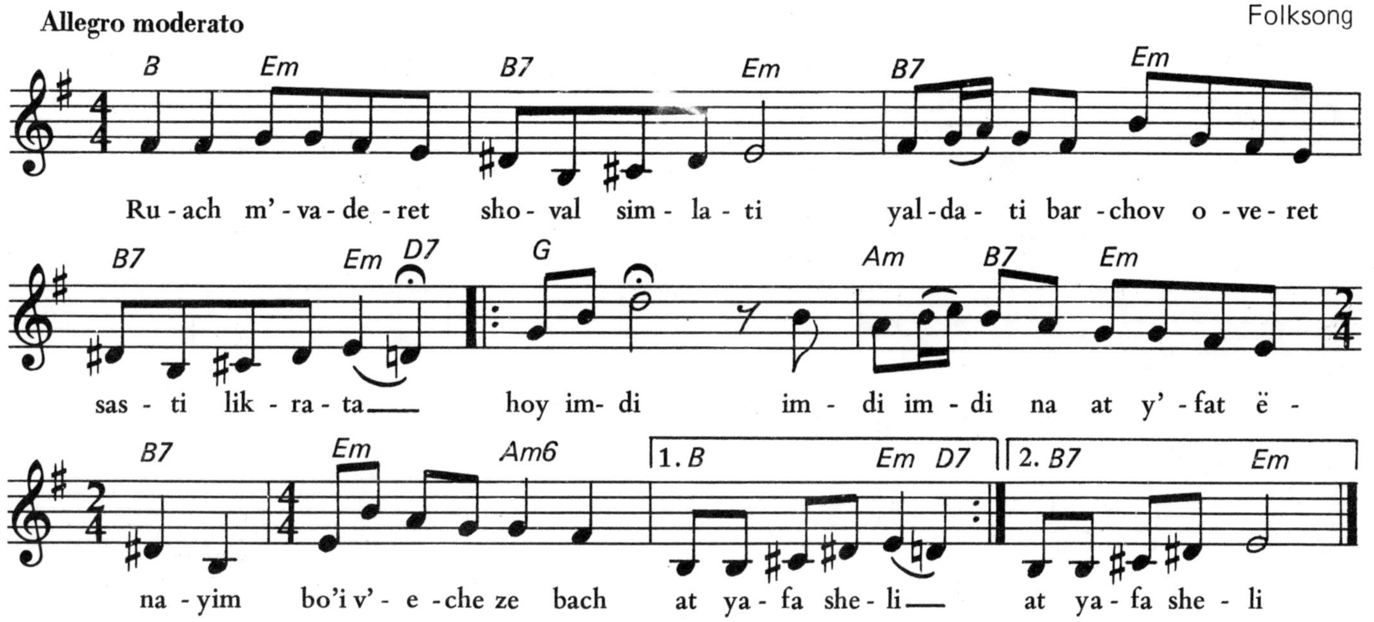

רוּחַ מְבַדֶּרֶת שׁוּבַל שִׂמְלָתָהּ,
יַלְדָּתִי בָּרְחוֹב עוֹבֶרֶת שַׂשְׂתִּי לִקְרָאתָהּ.
הוֹי עִמְדִי, עִמְדִי, נָא אַתְּ יְפַת עֵינַיִם,
בּוֹאִי וְאֶחֱזֶה בָּךְ אַתְּ יָפָה שֶׁלִּי.

Ruach m'va-de-ret sho-val sim-la-ta
Yal-da-ti bar-chov o-veret sas-ti lik-rata
Hoy imdi, imdi, na at y'fat ë-na-yim
Bo-i v'e-che-ze bach at ya-fa sheli

The wind rustles the sleeve of her dress,
In the street my child passes and I go to her in joy.
O stop, I ask you fair-eyed child,
Come, let me behold you, my beauty.

ELAD

Avraham Zigman, A. Zigman

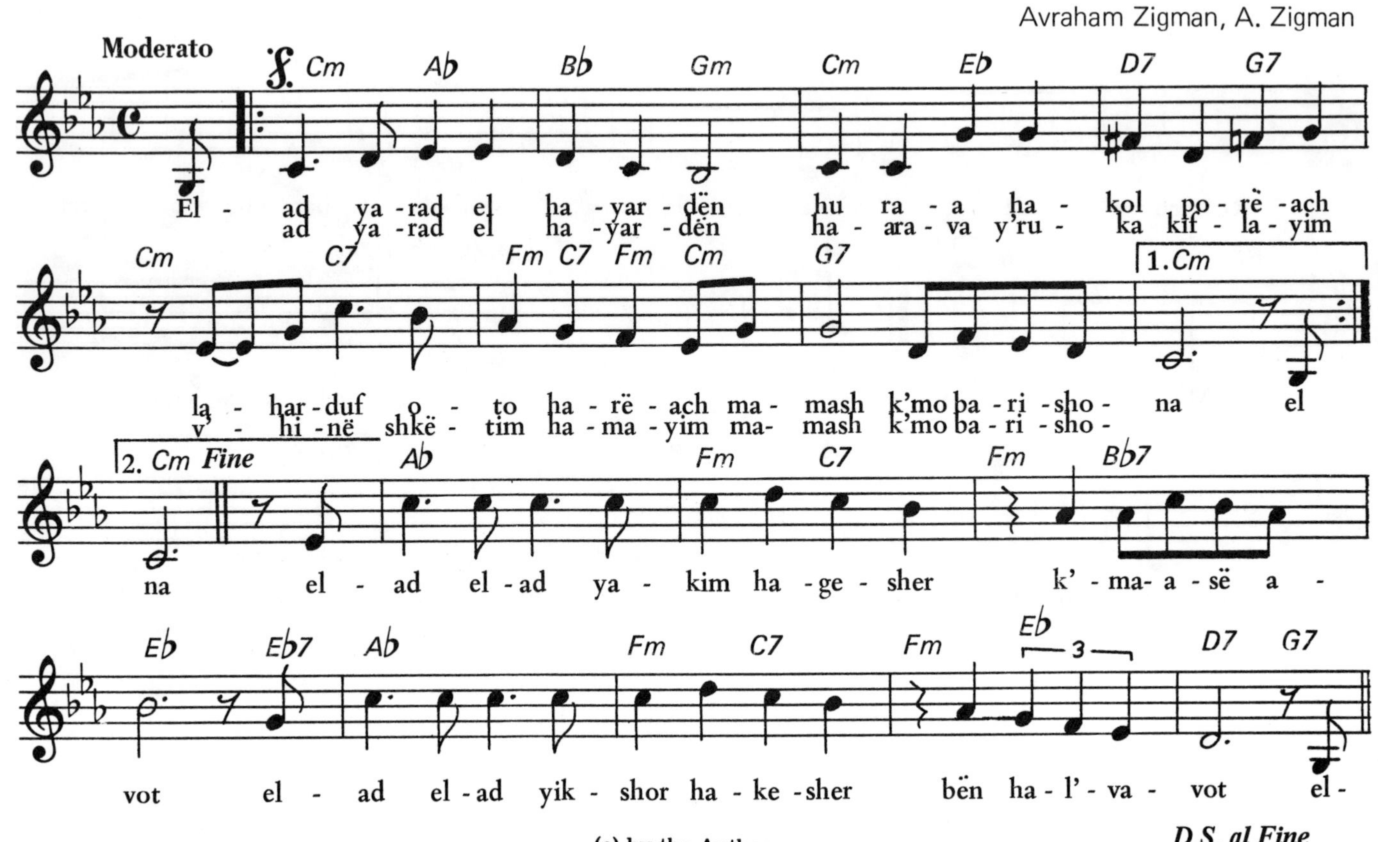

Elad yarad el ha-yar-dën
Hu ra-a ha-kol po-rë-ach
La-har-duf o-to ha-rë-ach
Ma-mash k'mo ba-ri-sho-na.

Elad yarad el ha-yar-dën
Ha-a-ra-va y'ru-ka kif-la-yim
V'hi-në shkëtim ha-ma-yim
Ma-mash k'mo ba-ri-sho-na

Chorus:

Elad, Elad yakim ha-ge-sher
K'ma-a-së avot
Elad, Elad yik-shor ha-ke-sher
Bën hal-va-vot.

אֶלְעָד יָרַד אֶל הַיַּרְדֵּן
הוּא רָאָה הַכֹּל פּוֹרֵחַ
לַהַרְדּוּף אוֹתוֹ הָרֵיחַ
מַמָּשׁ כְּמוֹ בָּרִאשׁוֹנָה.

אֶלְעָד יָרַד אֶל הַיַּרְדֵּן
הָעֲרָבָה יְרֻקָּה כִּפְלַיִם
וְהִנֵּה שְׁקֵטִים הַמַּיִם
מַמָּשׁ כְּמוֹ בָּרִאשׁוֹנָה.

פִּזְמוֹן:
אֶלְעָד, אֶלְעָד יָקִים הַגֶּשֶׁר
כְּמַעֲשֵׂה אָבוֹת
אֶלְעָד, אֶלְעָד יִקְשֹׁר הַקֶּשֶׁר
בֵּין הַלְּבָבוֹת.

Elad went down to the Jordan and saw everything in flower. The Oleander had the same aroma just as before. Elad went down to the Jordan. The plain was twice as green and the water was quiet as before. Elad will put up a bridge as did the fathers. Elad will tie the knot between the hearts.

YONA PAAMONA

Folksong

שָׁם הַרְחֵק עַל הַגִּבְעָה
אֹהָלִים שָׁם אַרְבָּעָה
זֶהוּ כָּל הַמַּחֲנֶה
כָּךְ נָאֶה וְכָךְ יָאֶה.
הֵי הֵי יוֹנָה, הֵי יוֹנָה פַּעֲמוֹנָה.

Sham harchëk al ha-giv-a
O-ha-lim sham ar-ba-a
Ze-hu kol ha-ma-cha-ne
Kach na-e v'chach ya-e
Hëy hëy yona pa-a-mo-na

Far away upon the hill four tents form a camp. It is a pleasant sight.

MA OMROT ENAYICH

She-mesh rad la-yam,
Ru-ach kal yë-hom.
Mi cho-lëm a-la-yich
B'mish-lat a-rom

Shnë o-rot ba-la-yil
Li rom-zim pit-om.
Ma omrot ë-na-yich
B'li lo-mar ad tom.

Bo-ker ët ya-or
Va-a-shuv mil-chom.
Ha-em-tza a-da-yin
Zë-cher la-cha-lom?

Bën sla-im va-har
Ëtz bo-dëd yi-nom
Mi ho-lëch ë-la-yich
Im a-rov ha-yom?

שֶׁמֶשׁ רַד לַיָּם,
רוּחַ קַל יֶהוֹם.
מִי חוֹלֵם עָלַיִךְ
בְּמִשְׁלַט עָרֹם

שְׁנֵי אוֹרוֹת בַּלַּיִל
לִי רוֹמְזִים פִּתְאֹם.
מָה אוֹמְרוֹת עֵינַיִךְ
בְּלִי לוֹמַר עַד תֹּם.

בֹּקֶר עֵת יָאוֹר
וְאָשׁוּב מִלְּחֹם.
הַאֶמְצָא עֲדַיִן
זֵכֶר לַחֲלוֹם?
שְׁנֵי אוֹרוֹת . .

בֵּין סְלָעִים וָהָר
עֵץ בּוֹדֵד יָנוֹם.
מִי הוֹלֵךְ אֵלַיִךְ
עִם עֲרֹב הַיּוֹם?
שְׁנֵי אוֹרוֹת . . .

The sun sets into the sea, a light wind blows. Who dreams of thee on a bleak plateau? Two lights in the night hint suddenly to me. What say your eyes without telling it all?

L'CHAYE HA-OLAM HA-ZE

Ha-am ha-ze ham-fu-lag kol ha-sha-na
Kë-tzad hu kam k'she-hu më-ri-ach sa-ka-na
Ëch mit-o-rër hu mi-nor-veg-ya v'ad chi-li
Ki hu yo-dë-a she– im ën ani li mi li
Ha ha...
L'cha-yë ha-am ha-ze, ha-am ha-ze
Ha-am ha-ze
She-ka-ma tov she-hu ka-ze
L'cha-yë ha-am ha-ze
She-ka-ma tov she-hu ka-ze

הָעָם הַזֶּה הַמְפֻלָּג כָּל הַשָּׁנָה
כֵּיצַד הוּא קָם כְּשֶׁהוּא מֵרִיחַ סַכָּנָה
אֵיךְ מִתְעוֹרֵר הוּא מִנּוֹרְבֶגְיָה וְעַד צִ׳ילִי.
כִּי הוּא יוֹדֵעַ שֶׁ — אִם אֵין אֲנִי לִי מִי לִי.
הַהַ . . .
לְחַיֵּי הָעָם הַזֶּה, הָעָם הַזֶּה,
הָעָם הַזֶּה,
שֶׁכָּמָה טוֹב שֶׁהוּא כָּזֶה
שֶׁהוּא כָּזֶה.
לְחַיֵּי הָעָם הַזֶּה
שֶׁכָּמָה טוֹב שֶׁהוּא כָּזֶה.

This nation is ever on guard and knows that it alone must protect itself. To the life of this wonderful nation!

SHNE SHOSHANIM

A-shir lach shir atik, no-shan
A-shir lach zemer al sho-shan,
Ha-yo ha-yu lif-në sha-nim
Shnë sho-sha-nim, shnë sho-sha-nim.
Ha-ya ze kvar, rachok ha-yom,
E-chad lavan, shë-ni adom.

אָשִׁיר לָךְ שִׁיר עַתִּיק, נוֹשָׁן,
אָשִׁיר לָךְ זֶמֶר עַל שׁוֹשָׁן,
הָיֹה הָיוּ לִפְנֵי שָׁנִים
שְׁנֵי שׁוֹשַׁנִּים, שְׁנֵי שׁוֹשַׁנִּים.
הָיָה זֶה כְּבָר, רָחוֹק הַיּוֹם,
אֶחָד לָבָן, שֵׁנִי אָדֹם.

Many years ago a red rose and a white rose flourished together in a garden. One day a hand plucked one and the heart of the other was broken.

AD OR HABOKER

Ad or ha-bo-ker
Ad sha-char y'natz-nëtz
She-chem el she-chem
So-ba ad ën këtz.

La-nu lëv e-chad,
E-shet y'tzu-ka,
Ya-chad b'ched-va,
Ya-chad bim-tzu-ka.

Ko-ach yësh– bit-cho-në-nu bo
Me-retz yësh– lo na-zuz mi-po!
Im a-yaf-nu– ba-nu ën ko-shël,
Hit-ro-faf-nu– nit-cha-shël!

עַד אוֹר הַבֹּקֶר,
עַד שַׁחַר יְנַצְנֵץ,
שֶׁכֶם אֶל שֶׁכֶם
סֹבָּה עַד אֵין קֵץ.

לָנוּ לֵב אֶחָד,
עֶשֶׁת יְצוּקָה,
יַחַד בְּחֶדְוָה,
יַחַד בִּמְצוּקָה.

כֹּחַ יֵשׁ — בִּטְחוֹנֵנוּ בּוֹ.
מֶרֶץ יֵשׁ — לֹא נָזוּז מִפֹּה!
אִם עָיַפְנוּ — בָּנוּ אֵין כּוֹשֵׁל,
הִתְרוֹפַפְנוּ — נִתְחַשֵּׁל!

Shoulder to shoulder we will dance the Hora until the break of day. Strength and energy are ours; we shall not fail.

KOLANIYOT

Nathan Alterman, Moshe Wilensky

Ha-e-rev ba, shki-a ba-har yo-ke-det.
A-ni cho-le-met v'ro-ot ë-nai:
Ha-gai-a na-a-ra k'ta-na yo-re-det
Uv-ësh ka-la-ni-ot lo-hët ha-gai.
Et ha-pra-chim litz-ror hi t'la-kët la,
U-vash-vi-lim ha-mit-ka-sim ba-tal
El i-ma hi nech-pe-zet v'ko-rët la:
'Ha-bi-ti ma hë-vë-ti lach ba-sal!'

Ka-la-ni-ot, ka-la-ni-ot, ka-la-ni-ot
A-dam-da-mot ad-mo-ni-yot
Ka-la-ni-ot, ka-la-ni-ot, ka-la-ni-ot
M'tu-la-lot chi-na-ni-yot
Shki-ot ba-har tiv-ar-na v'tid-ach-na,
A-val ta-mid ka-la-ni-ot tif-rach-na.
Su-fot la-rov të-hom-na v'tis-ar-na,
Ach më-cha-dash ka-la-ni-ot tiv-ar-na.
Ka-la-ni-ot, ka-la-ni-ot, ka-la-ni-ot
A-dam-da-mot ad-mo-ni-yot.

הָעֶרֶב בָּא, שְׁקִיעָה בָּהָר יוֹקֶדֶת.
אֲנִי חוֹלֶמֶת וְרוֹאוֹת עֵינַי:
הַגַּיְאָה נַעֲרָה קְטַנָּה יוֹרֶדֶת,
וּבְאֵשׁ כַּלָּנִיּוֹת לוֹהֵט הַגַּיְא.
אֶת הַפְּרָחִים לִצְרוֹר הִיא תְּלַקֵּט לָהּ,
וּבַשְּׁבִילִים הַמִּתְכַּסִּים בַּטַּל,
אֶל אִמָּא הִיא נֶחְפֶּזֶת וְקוֹרֵאת לָהּ:
׳הַבִּיטִי מָה הֵבֵאתִי לָךְ בַּסַּל!׳

כַּלָּנִיּוֹת, כַּלָּנִיּוֹת, כַּלָּנִיּוֹת אֲדַמְדַּמּוֹת אַדְמוֹנִיּוֹת.
כַּלָּנִיּוֹת, כַּלָּנִיּוֹת, כַּלָּנִיּוֹת מְטֻלָּלוֹת חִנָּנִיּוֹת.
שְׁקִיעוֹת בָּהָר תִּבְעַרְנָה וְתִדְעַכְנָה,
אֲבָל תָּמִיד כַּלָּנִיּוֹת תִּפְרַחְנָה.
סוּפוֹת לָרֹב תְּהֹמֶינָה וְתִסְעַרְנָה,
אַךְ מֵחָדָשׁ כַּלָּנִיּוֹת תִּבְעַרְנָה.
כַּלָּנִיּוֹת, כַּלָּנִיּוֹת, כַּלָּנִיּוֹת אֲדַמְדַּמּוֹת אַדְמוֹנִיּוֹת.

Evening comes, sunset burns in the mountain. I am dreaming and my eyes see: A small girl descending to the valley, and in a flame of Anemones the valley glows. She gathers the flowers into a boquet. And in the paths covered with dew she hurries to mother and calls out, Look at the basket I've brought you.

SHIR SAME-ACH

Yacov Orland, Mordechai Zeira

אִם גַּם רֹאשֵׁנוּ שַׁח
וְעֶצֶב סוֹבְבָנוּ —
הָבָה וְנִתְלַקַּח
מִן הַשִּׂמְחָה שֶׁבָּנוּ

הַי, הַי
הָבָה וְנִתְמַלֵּא
שִׂמְחָה שִׂמְחָה כִּמְלֹא הָעַיִן
הַי, הַי
שִׁירוּ עֲלֵה, עֲלֵה,
עֲלֵה וּבְעַר הַיַּיִן!
הַי, הַי . . .

Im gam ro-shë-nu shach
V'e-tzev so-v'-va-nu
Ha-va v'nit-la-kach
Min ha-sim-cha she-ba-nu

Hai, hai
Ha-va v'nit-ma-lë
Simcha simcha kim-lo ha-ayin
Hai, hai
Shiru a-lë, a-lë
A-lë uv-ar ha-ya-yin!
Hai, hai...

Though we be surrounded by despair,
let us rejoice and be happy.

EN GEDI

A. Peretz, D. Aharoni

Yam ha-ma-vet ha-ka-chol ba-lat ya-nu-a
U-mi-ma-al a-na-na k'ta-na ta-shut.
Ëtz ha-ë-shel bid-ma-ma ya-zu-a
V'chol kav bachol ya-fe cha-rut.
Ha-a-da-ma tatz-hiv b'la-hat she-mesh
V'a-vak ma-cha-nik ya-uf ba-rum,
Ach ën gedi lo tis-bol ba-ke-mesh
Ba yish-lot ga-ven ya-rok ya-chum

Ën gedi, ën gedi,
Me ha-ya ki tza-macht ba-cha-ma
Ën gedi, ën gedi,
Ëch pla-gim bach chot-rim bash-ma-ma.
Bach ha-yo-fi yo-fa b'chol hod
V'ha-lëv y'har-hër v'ya-cha-mod.

יַם־הַמָּוֶת הַכָּחֹל בַּלָּאט יָנוּעַ
וּמִמַּעַל עֲנָנָה קְטַנָּה תָּשׁוּט.
עֵץ הָאֵשֶׁל בִּדְמָמָה יָזוּעַ
וְכָל קַו בַּחוֹל יָפֶה חָרוּט.
הָאֲדָמָה תַּצְהִיב בְּלַהַט שֶׁמֶשׁ
וְאָבָק מַחֲנִיק יָעוּף בָּרוּם,
אַךְ עֵין־גֶּדִי לֹא תִּסְבֹּל בַּכֶּמֶשׁ
בָּהּ יִשְׁלֹט גָּוֶן יָרֹק יָחוּם.

עֵין־גֶּדִי, עֵין־גֶּדִי,
מֶה הָיָה כִּי צָמַחְתְּ בַּחַמָּה.
עֵין־גֶּדִי, עֵין־גֶּדִי,
אֵיךְ פְּלָגִים בָּךְ חוֹתְרִים בַּשְּׁמָמָה.
עֵין־גֶּדִי, עֵין־גֶּדִי,
בָּךְ הַיֹּפִי יוֹפַע בְּכָל הוֹד
וְהַלֵּב יְהַרְהֵר וְיַחְמֹד.

The blue Dead Sea quietly moves, and above a small cloud floats. A Terepinth silently sways and every line in the sand is well marked. The ground yellows in the heat of the sun, and the choking dust flies up. But Ein Gedi will not suffer wilting, in her a warm green hue will prevail.

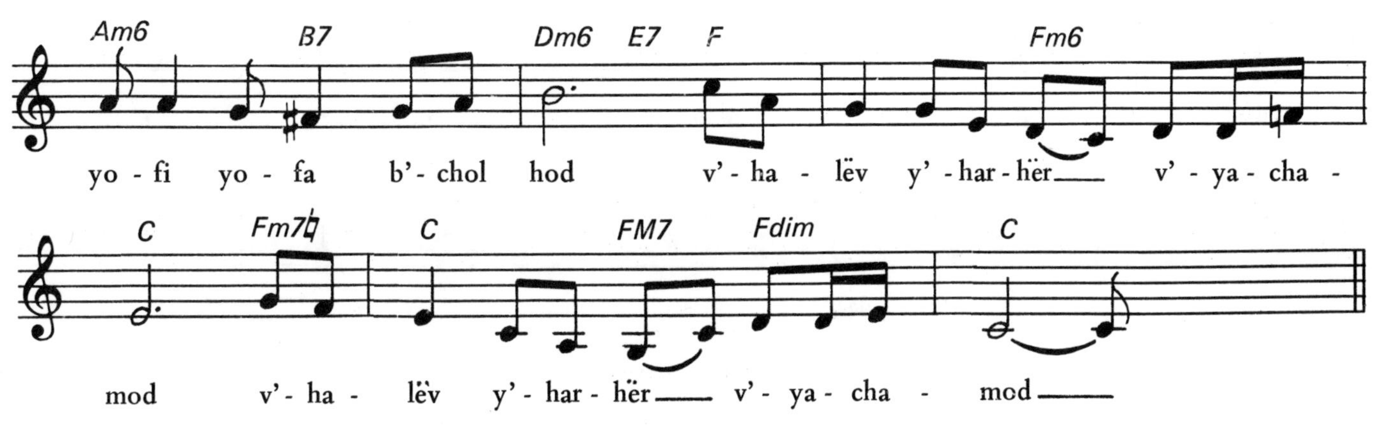

NAARA USH'MA KINNERET

Amos Ettinger, Dov Seltzer

לְרַגְלָיו שֶׁל הָהָר, לְחוֹפוֹ שֶׁל נָהָר
הִיא יוֹשְׁבָה לְבַדָּהּ, הֲתֵדְעוּ מַה סוֹדָהּ?
הַיַּרְדֵּן אָז שָׁתַק, הַחֶרְמוֹן שׁוּב צָחַק,
רַק סִפְּרָה הַשְּׁתִיקָה כִּי הִיא לוֹ מְחַכָּה.
אָז רַחַשׁ־יַרְדֵּן בֶּחָלָל עוֹד נִשְׁמַע
וְרַחַשׁ בִּכְיָה שֶׁל יַלְדָּה, אֲשֶׁר שְׁמָהּ . . .

כִּנֶּרֶת, כִּנֶּרֶת, כִּנֶּרֶת,
הָרוּחַ לָךְ שָׁר, הָרוּחַ לָךְ שָׁר,
וְשֶׁמֶשׁ יַרְדֵּן לָךְ זוֹהֶרֶת,
שׁוֹקַעַת בָּהָר, בָּהָר.

L'rag-lav shel ha-har, l'chofo shel na-har
Hi yosh-va l'va-da, ha-tëd'u ma so-da?
Ha-yar-dën az sha-tak, ha-cher-mon shuv tzachak,
Rak sip-ra hash-ti-ka ki hi lo m'cha-ka.
Az ra-chash-yardën be-cha-lal od nish-ma
V'rachash bich-ya shel yal-da, asher sh'ma...

Kineret, kineret, kineret,
Ha-ru-ach lach shar, ha-ru-ach lach shar,
V'she-mesh yardën lach zoheret,
Sho-ka-at ba-har, ba-har.

At the foot of the mountain on the shore of the river, she dwells alone. Do you know her secret? The Jordan was silent, Hermon laughed anew. Only the silence has told that she waits for him. The sound of the Jordan in the void still heard and the sound of the weeping girl whose name is.......... Kinneret, Kinneret, the wind sings to you, and the sun of the Jordan shines for you, setting in the mountain.

DABER ELAI BIFRACHIM

Uri Asaf, Dov Seltzer

בַּחֹרֶף הַגֶּשֶׁם דָּפַק עַל הַגַּג,
אָמְרָה כִּי לָבָן הוּא צִבְעָהּ הָאָהוּב.
לְיָד אָז הִגִּישׁ לָהּ — בַּלֵּב הָיָה חַג —
צְרוֹר נַרְקִיסִים רֵיחָנִי וְרָטֹב.

צַחֲקָה: נַעֲרִי הֶחָבִיב,
עוֹד נָשׁוּב נְדַבֵּר בָּאָבִיב.
דַּבֵּר אֵלַי בִּפְרָחִים, אֲהוּבִי,
דַּבֵּר אֵלַי בִּפְרָחִים.

אָבִיב בָּא; בִּקְשָׁה אֲבִיבִית לִהְיוֹת,
הוֹרִיקוּ שָׂדוֹת בַּמֶּרְחָב וּבַנִּיר.
הֵבִיא לָהּ זֵרִים צְהֻבֵּי חַרְצִיּוֹת,
אַךְ הִיא כְּבָר צִפְּתָה לְיוֹם קַיִץ בָּהִיר.

אֶת פִּרְחֵי הַתֵּבֵל לִי אֶאֱסֹף,
נִתְרָאֶה עֵת אָבִיב יַחֲלֹף.
דַּבֵּר אֵלַי בִּפְרָחִים אֲהוּבִי,
דַּבֵּר אֵלַי בִּפְרָחִים.

Ba-cho-ref ha-ge-shem da-fak al ha-gag,
Am-ra ki la-van hu tziv-a ha-a-huv.
La-yad az hi-gish la— ba-lëv ha-ya chag—
Tzror nar-ki-sim rë-cha-ni v'ra-tov

Tza-cha-ka: na-a-ri he-cha-viv
Od na-shuv n'da-bër ba-a-viv.
Da-bër ë-lai bif-ra-chim, a-hu-vi
Da-bër ë-lai bif-ra-chim.

Aviv ba; bik-sha a-vi-vit li-yot,
Ho-ri-ku sa-dot ba-mer-chav u-va-nir
Hë-vi la zë-rim tz'hu-bë char-tzi-yot,
Ach hi kvar tzip-ta l'yom ka-yitz ba-hir

Et pir-chë ha-të-vël li e-sof,
Nit-ra-e ët a-viv ya-cha-lof.
Da-bër ë-lai bif-ra-chim a-hu-vi
Da-bër ë-lai bif-ra-chim.

Speak to me with flowers, my beloved, speak to me with flowers.

CHOFIM

Nathan Yonathan, Nachum Heiman

Chofim hëm lif-a-mim ga-gu-im l'na-chal
Ra-i-ti pa-am chof she-na-chal a-za-vo
Im lëv sha-vur shel chol va-e-ven
V'ha-a-dam, v'ha-a-dam
Hu lif-a-mim gam kën ya-chol l'hi-sha-ër
Na-tush uv'li ko-chot ma-mash k'mo chof
Af hatz-da-fim k'mo chofim k'mo ha-ru-ach
Gam hatz-da-fim hëm lif-a-mim ga-gu-im
L'va-yit she-ta-mid a-hav-nu
Asher ha-ya v'rak ha-yam
Shar l'va-do sham et shirav.
Kach bën tzid-fë li-bo shel ha-a-dam
Sha-rim lo n'u-rav.

חוֹפִים הֵם לִפְעָמִים גַּעְגּוּעִים לְנַחַל.
רָאִיתִי פַּעַם חוֹף שֶׁנַּחַל עֲזָבוֹ
עִם לֵב שָׁבוּר שֶׁל חוֹל וָאֶבֶן
וְהָאָדָם, וְהָאָדָם
הוּא לִפְעָמִים גַּם־כֵּן יָכוֹל לְהִשָּׁאֵר
נָטוּשׁ וּבְלִי כֹּחוֹת
מַמָּשׁ כְּמוֹ חוֹף.

אַף הַצְּדָפִים כְּמוֹ חוֹפִים כְּמוֹ הָרוּחַ
גַּם הַצְּדָפִים הֵם לִפְעָמִים גַּעְגּוּעִים
לְבַיִת שֶׁתָּמִיד אָהַבְנוּ,
אֲשֶׁר הָיָה וְרַק הַיָּם
שָׁר לְבַדּוֹ שָׁם אֶת שִׁירָיו. כָּךְ בֵּין צִדְפֵּי
לִבּוֹ שֶׁל הָאָדָם
שָׁרִים לוֹ נְעוּרָיו.

Sometimes shores are yearnings for a stream. Once I saw a shore which a stream had left with a broken heart of sand and stone. Sometimes a man can also remain forelorn and powerless, just like a shore.

YESH P'RACHIM

Nathan Yonathan, Moni Amariglio

(c) by the Authors

Ha-ra-i-ta ë-ze yo-fi
She-ra-ad b'ru-ach stav–
S'dë za-hav da-ach ba-o-fel
V'hid-lik në-rot cha-tzav.

Ha-ra-i-ta ë-ze o-dem
She-tza-ak la-mer-cha-kim
S'dë da-mim ha-ya sham ko-dem
V'ach-shav hu s'dë p'ra-gim.

Al tik-tof na-a-ri
Yësh pra-chim she-b'në cha-lof
Yësh pra-chim she-ad ën sof
Nish-a-rim ba-man-gi-na

Al tik-tof na-a-ri
Yësh pra-chim she-b'në cha-lof
Yësh pra-chim she-ad ën sof
Im ha-man-gi-na...

הֲרָאִיתָ אֵיזֶה יֹפִי
שֶׁרָעַד בְּרוּחַ סְתָו —
שְׂדֵה זָהָב דָּעַךְ בָּאֹפֶל
וְהִדְלִיק נֵרוֹת חָצָב.

הֲרָאִיתָ אֵיזֶה אֹדֶם
שֶׁצָּעַק לַמֶּרְחַקִּים
שְׂדֵה דָּמִים הָיָה שָׁם קֹדֶם
וְעַכְשָׁו הוּא שְׂדֵה פְּרָגִים.

אַל תִּקְטֹף, נַעֲרִי
יֵשׁ פְּרָחִים שֶׁבְּנֵי חֲלוֹף
יֵשׁ פְּרָחִים שֶׁעַד אֵין סוֹף
נִשְׁאָרִים בַּמַּנְגִּינָה.

אַל תִּקְטֹף נַעֲרִי
יֵשׁ פְּרָחִים שֶׁבְּנֵי חֲלוֹף
יֵשׁ פְּרָחִים שֶׁעַד אֵין סוֹף
עִם הַמַּנְגִּינָה . . .

Have you seen the beauty which trembled in the autumn wind– A golden field flickered in darkness and lit the candles of Chatzav. Have you seen the redness which cried out to the distance, a bloody field was there before and now a field of poppies. Don't pick them my child. There are flowers which pass away, there are flowers which stay forever in the melody.

BISHARAYICH Y'RUSHALAYIM

Y. Gamzu, Y. Braun

עוֹמְדוֹת רַגְלֵינוּ בִּשְׁעָרַיִךְ, יְרוּשָׁלַיִם,
וְתוֹתָחֵינוּ מַרְעִימִים לָךְ שִׁיר־מִזְמוֹר.
וְרַק דִּמְעוֹת־הַגַּאֲוָה שֶׁבָּעֵינַיִם
נוֹטְפוֹת דּוּמָם, עַל הַמַּדִּים וְהֶחָגוֹר . . .

צִיּוֹן, הֲלֹא תִשְׁאֲלִי לִשְׁלוֹם בַּחוּרַיִךְ.
צִיּוֹן, זֶה הָאשֶׁר שׁוֹאֵג בְּחָזֵנוּ, פִּרְאִי.
לַמְנַצֵּחַ מִזְמוֹר עַל מִקְלָע וְרִמּוֹן בִּשְׁעָרַיִךְ —
בְּדָמֵנוּ חַיִּי,
בְּדָמֵנוּ חַיִּי . . .

מִשֵּׁיךְ גַּ׳רַאח עַד נֶבִּי־סַמוּאֶל, לַיִל־לַיִל,
הָיוּ רוּחוֹת־תַּשַׁ״ח שָׁרוֹת לָךְ, בְּדַרְכָּן:
״אִם אֶשְׁכָּחֵךְ . . . אִם אֶשְׁכָּחֵךְ, יְרוּשָׁלַיִם . . .״
אַךְ לֹא שָׁכַחְנוּ — וַהֲרֵי אֲנַחְנוּ כָּאן!

צִיּוֹן, הֲלֹא תִשְׁאֲלִי . . .

Omdot rag-lënu bish-a-ra-yich Y'rushalayim
V'to-ta-chë-nu mar-i-mim lach shir mizmor.
V'rak dim-ot- ha-ga-a-va she-ba-ë-nayim
Not-fot du-mam, al hamadim v'he-cha-gor...

Tziyon, ha-lo tish-a-li lish-lom ba-chu-ra-yich.
Tziyon, ze ha-o-sher sho-ëg b'cha-zë-nu, pir-i.
Lam-na-tzë-ach mizmor al mik-la v'rimon bish-a-rayich–
B'da-më-nu cha-yi,
B'da-më-nu cha-yi...

Mi-shëch, ja-rach ad Nebi Samuel, layil-layil,
Ha-yu ru-chot-ta-shach sha-rot lach, b'darkan:
"Im esh-ka-chëch...im esh-ka-chëch, Y'rushalayim..."
Ach lo sha-chach-nu– va-ha-rë anachnu kan!

Tziyon, ha-lo tish-a-li...

We stand at the gates of Jerusalem and our cannons roar your praise.
We have not forgotten thee Jerusalem.....

HAYU Z'MANIM

Haim Hefer, Moshe Wilensky
Andante
Dm Em A7
Ya - vo ha- yom v' - od të-shëv el mul ha - ach v' -gam ha -
Gm A7 Dm A7 Dm F
gav yi-ye ka-fuf ka-cha-to - te -ret v'-ti-za- chër az b'-ya-me-cha ba-pal -
Gm Gm7 C7 F
mach u-t'-sa-për al zot a-gav i-shun mik- te -ret u-mi-sa
Dm6 E7 Am D7
viv u-mi-sa-viv yë-shëv ha- taf v'-ish-t'- cha gam hi muf-le-get b'-sha -
Gm Dm Gm
nim ta-zil dim- a u-t' - ka-në - ach et ha -
D7 Gm E7 Em A7
af v'-të - a- nach ha-yu zma-nim ha-yu zma -
Dm Am7 D7 Gm C7
nim ha-yu zma- nim az ba-mish-lat ya- shav-nu ha-yu zma -
F C7 F Dm Em7
nim la-cham-nu v' - a - hav - nu ach-shav da - var ën l'-ha-kir al ha-mish -

Ya-vo hayom v'od të-shëv el mul ha-ach,
V'gam ha-gav yi-ye ka-fuf ka-cha-to-te-ret
V'ti-za-chër az b'ya-me-cha ba-palmach,
Ut'sa-për al zot agav i-shun mik-te-ret

U-mi-sa-viv u-mi-sa-viv yë-shëv ha-taf
V'ish-t'cha gam hi muf-le-get b'sha-nim
Ta-zil dim-a ut-ka-në-ach et ha-af,
V'të-a-nach: hayu z'manim, hayu z'manim...

Hayu z'manim,
Az ba-mishlat ya-shav-nu,
Hayu z'manim
La-cham-nu v'ahav-nu,
Achshav davar ën l'ha-kir—
Al hamish-lat yo-she-vet ir
U-lai biz-chut o-tam z'manim...

יָבוֹא הַיּוֹם וְעוֹד תֵּשֵׁב אֶל מוּל הָאָח,
וְגַם הַגַּב יִהְיֶה כָּפוּף כַּחֲטוֹטֶרֶת
וְתִזָּכֵר אָז בְּיָמֶיךָ בַּפַּלְמַ״ח,
וּתְסַפֵּר עַל זֹאת אַגַּב עִשּׁוּן מִקְטֶרֶת.

וּמִסָּבִיב וּמִסָּבִיב יֵשֵׁב הַטַּף,
וְאִשְׁתְּךָ גַּם הִיא מֻפְלֶגֶת בְּשָׁנִים
תַּזִּיל דִּמְעָה וּתְקַנֵּחַ אֶת הָאַף,
וְתֵאָנַח: הָיוּ זְמַנִּים, הָיוּ זְמַנִּים . . .

הָיוּ זְמַנִּים,
אָז בַּמִּשְׁלָט יָשַׁבְנוּ,
הָיוּ זְמַנִּים
לָחַמְנוּ וְאָהַבְנוּ,
עַכְשָׁו דָּבָר אֵין לְהַכִּיר —
עַל הַמִּשְׁלָט יוֹשֶׁבֶת עִיר
אוּלַי בִּזְכוּת אוֹתָם זְמַנִּים . . .

A time will come when your days in the Palmach will be but a memory. You will sigh, "those were the days..........."

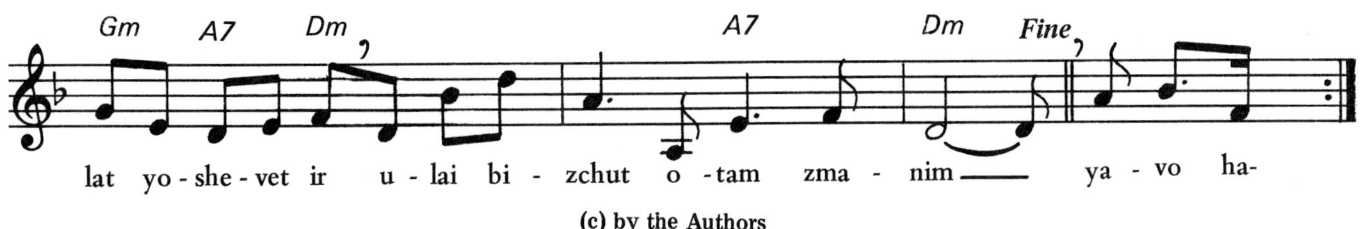

ELI, ELI

Ëli, she-lo yi-ga-mër l'olam
Hachol v'hayam
Rishrush shel ha-ma-yim
B'rak ha-sha-ma-yim
T'filat ha-a-dam

אֵלִי, שֶׁלֹּא יִגָּמֵר לְעוֹלָם
הַחוֹל וְהַיָּם,
רִשְׁרוּשׁ שֶׁל הַמַּיִם,
בְּרַק הַשָּׁמַיִם,
תְּפִלַּת הָאָדָם.

**My God, let there never be an end to the sand an the sea,
the ocean's roar, the sparkling skies, the prayer of man.**

MA YAFIM HALELOT

Oriental Folksong

מַה יָּפִים הַלֵּילוֹת בִּכְנַעַן,
צוֹנְנִים הֵם וּבְהִירִים,
הַדְּמָמָה פָּלְטָה שִׁיר,
יַעַן לָהּ לִבִּי בְּשִׁירָה.

פִּזְמוֹן:
יִלְלַת תַּנִּים נוּגָה
תֶּחֱצֶה דְּמִי הַלַּיִל.

Ma yafim ha-lë-lot bich-na-an
Tzo-n'nim hëm uv'hi-rim
Had'ma-ma pal-ta shir
Ya-an la li-bi v'shi-ra
Y'lilat tanim nu-ga
Te-che-tze d'mi ha-la-yil

How beautiful are the nights in Canaan cool and clear, The silence bursts forth in song, my heart will answer in singing. The wail of the jackal is mournful, splitting the silence of the night.

BEN N'HAR P'RAT

C.N.Bialik, Oriental Folktune

Bĕn n'har prat un'har chi-de-kel
Al ha-har mi-ta-mĕr de-kel
U-va-de-kel, bĕn a-fa-av
Tish-kon la du-chi-fat za-hav.

Tzi-por za-hav! U-fi chu-gi,
Tz'i u-vak-shi li ben zu-gi
Uva-a-sher tim-tza-i-hu
Kif-ti o-to va-ha-vi-i-hu.

בֵּין נְהַר פְּרָת וּנְהַר חִדֶּקֶל
עַל הָהָר מִתַּמֵּר דֶּקֶל
וּבַדֶּקֶל, בֵּין עֲפָאָיו
תִּשְׁכֹּן לָהּ דּוּכִיפַת זָהָב.

צִפּוֹר זָהָב! עוּפִי חוּגִי,
צְאִי וּבַקְּשִׁי לִי בֶּן־זוּגִי
וּבַאֲשֶׁר תִּמְצָאִיהוּ
כַּפְתִּי אוֹתוֹ וַהֲבִיאִיהוּ.

Between the Euphrates and the Tigris on a mountain flourishes the Palm tree and between its palms dwells a golden peacock.

AHAVAT HADASSAH

Oriental Folktune

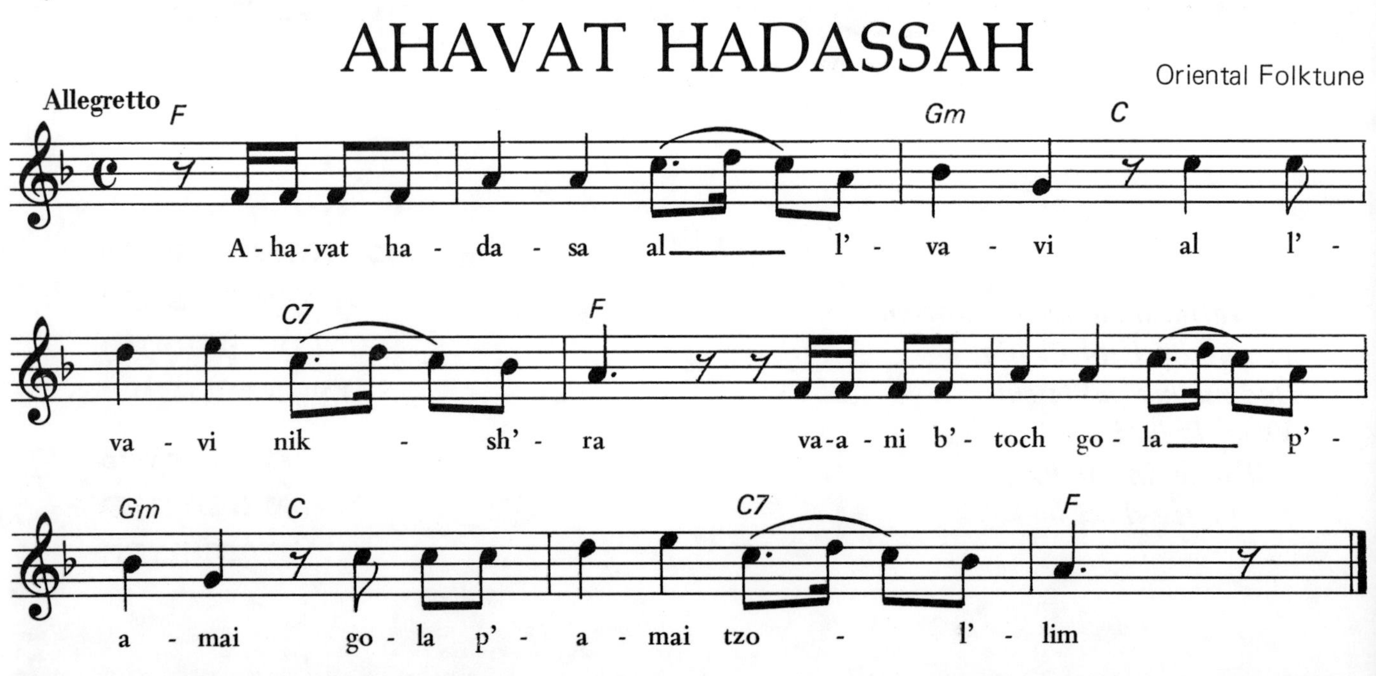

A-ha-vat ha-da-sa al l'va-vi nik-sh'ra
Va-a-ni b'toch go-la p'a-mai tzo-l'-lim

אַהֲבַת הֲדַסָּה עַל לְבָבִי נִקְשְׁרָה.
וַאֲנִי בְּתוֹךְ גּוֹלָה פְּעָמַי צוֹלְלִים.

The love of Zion is bound securely to my heart. But alas I am in the diaspora.

HITRAG'UT

Im yësh ë-sham rachok na-ve ka-tan sha-kët
V'lo g'zuz-t'ra shel ëtz v'al ya-da sha-këd
Im yësh ë-sham rachok v'lo më-ot par-sa
Sav-ta l'nech-da-ta tashir ar-se-cha
Ki az a-uf l'sham b'a-chad ha-a-ra-vim
V'shuv nim-ne yach-dav mis-par ha-ko-cha-vim

אִם יֵשׁ אֵי־שָׁם רָחוֹק נָוֶה קָטָן שָׁקֵט
וְלוֹ גְזוּזְטְרָה שֶׁל עֵץ וְעַל יָדָהּ שָׁקֵד

אִם יֵשׁ אֵי־שָׁם רָחוֹק וְלוֹ מֵאוֹת פַּרְסָה
סַבְתָּה לְנֶכְדָּתָהּ תָּשִׁיר עַרְשֵׁךְ

כִּי אָז אָעוּף לְשָׁם בְּאַחַד הָעֲרָבִים
וְשׁוּב נִמְנֶה יַחְדָּו מִסְפַּר הַכּוֹכָבִים.

In a far distant land stands a quiet little dwelling. There a grandmother sings a cradle song to her little one— I would fly there one evening and count the stars with her.

MI YITNENI OF

מִי יִתְּנֵנִי עוֹף צִפּוֹר כְּנַף קְטַנָּה
הָהּ, בִּנְדוּדַי אֵין סוֹף נַפְשִׁי מַה מִּתְעַנָּה.

Mi yit-në-ni of tzipor ka-naf k'ta-na
Ha, bin-du-dë ën sof nafshi ma mit-a-na

Who will give me wings, even wings of the smallest bird?
Endlessly will I wander to find place for my wounded soul.

KI ESHM'RA SHABBAT*

Z'mirot Liturgy
Oriental Folksong

Ki esh-m'ra Shabbat Ël yish-m'rëni
Ot hi l'ol-më ad bë-no u-vë-ni

כִּי אֶשְׁמְרָה שַׁבָּת אֵל יִשְׁמְרֵנִי
אוֹת הִיא לְעוֹלְמֵי עַד
בֵּינוֹ וּבֵינִי.

If I safeguard the Sabbath, God will safeguard me. It is a sign forever between Him and me.

** Also known as AHAVAT HADASSAH.*
See Israel in Song page 71.

MIZMOR L'DAVID

Liturgy
Sephardic Folktune

מִזְמוֹר לְדָוִד: הָבוּ לַייָ בְּנֵי אֵלִים הָבוּ לַייָ כָּבוֹד וָעֹז
הָבוּ לַייָ כְּבוֹד שְׁמוֹ הִשְׁתַּחֲווּ לַייָ בְּהַדְרַת קֹדֶשׁ
קוֹל יְיָ עַל הַמָּיִם אֵל הַכָּבוֹד הִרְעִים יְיָ עַל מַיִם רַבִּים
קוֹל יְיָ בַּכֹּחַ

Mizmor l'david: Havu Ladonai b'nē ē-lim Havu Ladonai kavod va-oz, havu Ladonai kavod sh'mo, hishtachavu Ladonai b'hadrat kodesh. Kol Adonai al ha-ma-yim, Ēl hakavod hir-im Adonai al mayim rabim kol Adonai ba-ko-ach.

A Psalm of David. Give to the Lord, O heavenly beings, give to the Lord honor and glory. Give to the Lord the glory due to His name; worship the Lord in holy array. The voice of the Lord is heard across the waters; it is the God of glory thundering!

YA RIBON

Z'mirot Liturgy
Folksong

יָהּ רִבּוֹן עָלַם וְעָלְמַיָּא.
אַנְתְּ הוּא מַלְכָּא מֶלֶךְ מַלְכַיָּא.
עוֹבַד גְּבוּרְתֵּךְ וְתִמְהַיָּא.
שְׁפַר קֳדָמָךְ לְהַחֲוָיָא.

Ya ribon a-lam v'al-ma-ya
Ant hu mal-ka me-lech mal-cha-ya
O-vad g'vur-tëch v'tim-ha-ya
Sh'far ko-da-mach l'ha-cha-va-ya

Master of the world and of all worlds, You are the King who reigns over all kings., it is wonderful to declare your powerful deeds.

YOM ZE L'YISRAEL

Z'mirot Liturgy
Sephardic Folksong

יום זֶה לְיִשְׂרָאֵל אוֹרָה וְשִׂמְחָה שַׁבָּת מְנוּחָה.

Yom ze l'yisraël ora v'simcha Shabbat m'nucha

This day is for Israel- a day of light and gladness, the Sabbath of rest.

D'ROR YIKRA

דְּרוֹר יִקְרָא לְבֵן עִם בַּת,
וְיִנְצָרְכֶם כְּמוֹ בָבַת,
נְעִים שִׁמְכֶם וְלֹא יֻשְׁבַּת,
שְׁבוּ וְנוּחוּ בְּיוֹם שַׁבָּת.

D'ror yikra l'vën im bat
V'yin-tzar-chem k'mo vavat
N'im shim-chem v'lo yushbat
Sh'vu v'nu-chu b'yom Shabbat

He shall proclaim freedom for all and protect you.
Rest and be contented on the Sabbath day.

SA-ENU

Sa-ënu, sa-ënu lamidbar sa-ënu
Cha-lila la-chem t'chal'lu
Ha-ro-im na-mim
U-va-lë-lot al hash-vi-lim
Ha-ko-cha-vim romzim
Sa-ënu, sa-ënu lamidbar sa-ënu

שָׂאֵנוּ שָׂאֵנוּ לַמִּדְבָּר שָׂאֵנוּ
חָלִילָה לָכֶם תְּחַלְּלוּ
הָרוֹעִים נָמִים
וּבַלֵּילוֹת עַל הַשְּׁבִילִים
הַכּוֹכָבִים רוֹמְזִים
שָׂאֵנוּ שָׂאֵנוּ לַמִּדְבָּר שָׂאֵנוּ

Carry us to the desert! Play on your flutes while shepherds doze. Carry us to the desert.

SCALERICA D'ORO

Ladino Folksong

Scalerica de oro, de oro y marfil
para que suva la novia a dar
kidduschin.

Venimos a ver, venimos a ver.
Y gozen y logren y tengan
muncho bien.

La novia no tiene dinero.
Que mos tenga un mazal bueno.
Venimos a ver........................

La novia no tiene contado.
Que mos tenga un mazal alto.
Venimos a ver.......................

A little ladder of gold and ivory,
so our little bride can go up to
take her marriage vows.

We've come to see, we've come to see.
May they have joy and prosper and
always be happy.

The bride has no money.
May they have good fortune.
We've come to see..............

The bride has no riches,
May they have good luck.
We've come to see..........

YO M'ENAMORI D'UN AIRE

Yo m'enamori d'un aire, ah—
d'un aire d'una mujer,
d'una mujer muy hermoza
linda de mi corason
Yo m'enamori d'un aire, ah—
Linda de mi corason
Tralala, lala.............
Linda de mi corason

Yo m'enamori de noche, ah—
el lunar ya m'engano.
Si esto era de dia,
yo no atava amor.
Yo m'enamori de noche, ah—
yo on atava amor.
Tralala, lala..........
yo no atava amor.

Si otra vez m'enamoro, ah—
d'un aire d'una mujer,
d'una mujer muy hermoza
linda de mi corason
Sea de dia con sol, ah—
si otra vez m'enamoro.
Sea de dia con sol.
Tralala, lala..........
Si otra vez m'enamoro,
sea de dia con sol.

I fell in love with the charms, oh—
the charms of a woman,
of a very beautiful woman,
the beauty of my heart.
I fell in love with the charms, oh—
the beauty of my heart.
Tralala, lala..................
The beauty of my heart.

I fell in love at night, oh—
the moonlight was my undoing.
If it had been in daylight,
Love would not have bound me.
I fell in love at night, oh—
love would not have bound me.
Tralala, lala.....................
love would not have bound me.

If again I fall in love, oh—
with the charms of a woman,
of a very beautiful woman,
the beauty of my heart.
It will be by day with sunshine, oh—
if again I fall in love.
It will be by day with sunshine, oh—
Tralalala, lala.....................
If again I fall in love
it will be by day with sunshine.

CUANDO EL REY NIMROD

Cuando el rey Nimrod
al campo salia,
mirava en el cielo
y en la estreyeria,
Vido una luz santa
en la giuderia,
que havia de nacer
Avraham avinu.
Avram avinu, padre querido
padre bendicho, luz de Israel.

Saludemos al compadre
y tambien al moel.
Que por su zekhut
mos venga el goel
y ri'hma a todo Israel.
Cierto loaremos al verdadero
al verdadero de Israel.

When King Nimrod
went out into the fields,
he looked at the heavens
and at all the stars,
He saw a holy light
above the Jewish quarter,
a sign that Abraham our father
was about to be born.
Abraham our father, beloved father,
blessed father, light of Israel.

Let us greet the godfather
and also the moel.
Because of his virtue
may the Messiah come
to redeem all Israel.
Surely we will praise the true redeemer
the true redeemer of Israel.

Also sung with the text of SHALOM ALECHEM
See Great Songs of Israel, page 36

LOS BILBILICOS*

Ladino Folksong

Los bilbilicos cantan
Con sospiros de amor;
Mi neshama mi ventura
Estan en tu poder.

La rosa enflorese
En el mes de mai
Mi neshama s'escuresе,
Sufriendo del amor.

Mas presto ven palomba
Mas presto ven con mi;
Mas presto ven querida,
Corre y salvame.

The nightingales sing
With sighs of love;
My soul and my fate
Are in your power.

The rose blooms
In the month of May.
My soul and my fate
Suffer from love's pain.

Come more quickly, dove,
More quickly come with me;
More quickly come, beloved,
Run and save me.

* *Also known as TZUR MISHELO.*
See Israel in Song page 42.

Y'DID NEFESH

Y'did nefesh av ha-ra-cha-man
M'shoch av-d'cha el r'tzo-ne-cha
Yarutz av-d'-cha k'mo ayal
Yish-ta-cha-ve el mul ha-da-re-cha
Ye-e-rav lo y'di-do-te-cha
Mi-no-fet tzuf v'chol ta-am

יְדִיד נֶפֶשׁ אָב הָרַחֲמָן
מְשׁוֹךְ עַבְדְּךָ אֶל רְצוֹנֶךָ
יָרוּץ עַבְדְּךָ כְּמוֹ אַיָּל
יִשְׁתַּחֲוֶה אֶל מוּל הֲדָרֶךָ
יֶעֱרַב לוֹ יְדִידוֹתֶיךָ
מִנֹּפֶת צוּף וְכָל טָעַם.

Beloved of the soul, Merciful Father, draw Thy servant unto Thy will, that swift as a hart he may run to prostrate himself before You.

Y'VARECH'CHA

Y'va-re-ch'-cha Hashem mi-tzi-yon
Ur'-ë b'tuv Y'ru-sha-la-yim
Kol y'më cha-ye-cha
Ur'-ë vanim l'va-ne-cha
Shalom al Yisraël

יְבָרֶכְךָ ה׳ מִצִּיּוֹן
וּרְאֵה בְּטוּב יְרוּשָׁלָיִם
כֹּל יְמֵי חַיֶּיךָ
וּרְאֵה בָנִים לְבָנֶיךָ
שָׁלוֹם עַל יִשְׂרָאֵל.

The Lord bless you from Zion; may you see the welfare of Jerusalem all the days of your life; may you live to see your children's children. Peace be upon Israel.

UVA-U HA-OVDIM

Isaiah 27:13
Music by Rabbi S. Carlebach

וּבָאוּ הָאוֹבְדִים בְּאֶרֶץ אַשּׁוּר וְהַנִּדָּחִים בְּאֶרֶץ מִצְרָיִם
וְהִשְׁתַּחֲווּ לה׳ בְּהַר הַקֹּדֶשׁ בִּירוּשָׁלָיִם.

U-va-u ha-ovdim b'eretz ashur
V'hanidachim b'eretz mitz-ra-yim
V'hishta-cha-vu Lashem b'har ha-ko-desh
Birushalayim

And they shall come that were lost in the land of Assyria, and they that were dispersed in the land of Egypt; and they shall worship the Lord at the holy mountain in Jerusalem.

V'KAREV P'ZURENU

וְקָרֵב פְּזוּרֵינוּ מִבֵּין הַגּוֹיִם, וּנְפוּצוֹתֵינוּ כַּנֵּס מִיַּרְכְּתֵי אָרֶץ.

V'ka-rëv p'zu-rënu mi-bën ha-go-yim un'fu-tzo-tënu ka-nës mi-yar-k'të aretz

Bring our scattered ones among the nations nearer unto Thee
and gather our dispersed from the ends of the earth.

UFARATZTA

וּפָרַצְתָּ יָמָּה וָקֵדְמָה
צָפוֹנָה וָנֶגְבָּה

Ufaratzta yama va-këd-ma
Tzafona va-neg-ba

And thou shalt spread forth to the west and to the east, to the north and to the south.

KETZAD M'RAKDIN

כֵּיצַד מְרַקְּדִין לִפְנֵי הַכַּלָּה
כַּלָּה נָאָה וַחֲסוּדָה.

Kë-tzad m'rak-din lif-në ha-ka-la
Ka-la na-a va-cha-su-da

What do we say while dancing before the bride?
The bride is beautiful and virtuous.

TALIT

Ti-na-tzël nafshi v'ruchi v'nish-mati
Ut-fi-la-ti min ha-chi-tzo-nim
V'ta-tzi-lëm k'nesher ya-ir kino
Al go-za-lav y'ra-chëf

תִּנָּצֵל נַפְשִׁי וְרוּחִי וְנִשְׁמָתִי וּתְפִלָּתִי מִן הַחִיצוֹנִים
וְתַצִּילֵם כְּנֶשֶׁר יָעִיר קִנּוֹ עַל גּוֹזָלָיו יְרַחֵף.

(And through the commandment of the fringes) shall be delivered my soul, and my spirit, and my prayer from outside evils; and may the Talit deliver them as an eagle that stirs up her nest and hovers over her young.

SHAVUA TOV

Sha-vu-a tov. שָׁבוּעַ טוֹב.

A good week! (Traditional greeting at the close of Sabbath.)

HAVA N'RAN'NA

With Hassidic fervor

ZEMER HASIDI

With movement

SIMAN TOV

Liturgy
Hassidic Folksong

Siman tov u-mazal tov y'hë lanu
U-l'chol Yisraël

סִימָן טוֹב וּמַזָּל טוֹב
יְהֵא לָנוּ וּלְכָל יִשְׂרָאֵל

Auspicious sign and good fortune may these be unto us and to all Israel.

SHALOM ALECHEM

שָׁלוֹם עֲלֵיכֶם מַלְאֲכֵי הַשָּׁרֵת מַלְאֲכֵי עֶלְיוֹן
מִמֶּלֶךְ מַלְכֵי הַמְּלָכִים הַקָּדוֹשׁ בָּרוּךְ הוּא.

בּוֹאֲכֶם לְשָׁלוֹם מַלְאֲכֵי הַשָּׁלוֹם מַלְאֲכֵי עֶלְיוֹן
מִמֶּלֶךְ מַלְכֵי הַמְּלָכִים הַקָּדוֹשׁ בָּרוּךְ הוּא.

בָּרְכוּנִי לְשָׁלוֹם . . .

צֵאתְכֶם לְשָׁלוֹם . . .

Shalom alëchem mal-a-chë ha-sha-rët mal-a-chë elyon
Mimelech mal-chë ham'lachim ha-ka-dosh baruch hu:
Bo-achem....Barchuni......Tzëtchem........

Peace be upon you, angels of the Exalted One, from the King of Kings, the Holy One blessed be He. May your coming be for the sake of peace. Bless me for peace; and may your departure as well be with peace.

YA RIBON

Z'mirot Liturgy
Folksong

יָהּ רִבּוֹן עָלַם וְעָלְמַיָּא.
אַנְתְּ הוּא מַלְכָּא מֶלֶךְ מַלְכַיָּא.
עוֹבַד גְּבוּרְתֵּךְ וְתִמְהַיָּא.
שְׁפַר קֳדָמָךְ לְהַחֲוָיָא.

Ya ribon a-lam v'al-ma-ya
Ant hu mal-ka me-lech mal-cha-ya
O-vad g'vur-tëch v'tim-ha-ya
Sh'far ko-da-mach l'ha-cha-va-ya

Master of the world and of all worlds, You are the King who reigns over all kings., it is wonderful to declare your powerful deeds.

TZUR MISHELO

Z'mirot Liturgy
Folksong

Tzur mi-she-lo achalnu bar'chu emu-nai
Sa-va-nu v'ho-tar-nu kidvar Adonai
Ha-zan et o-la-mo ro-ë-nu avinu
Achalnu et lachmo v'yë-no sha-ti-nu
Al kën no-de lish-mo un'hal'lo b'finu
Amarnu v'aninu ën kadosh ka-do-nai

צוּר מִשֶּׁלּוֹ אָכַלְנוּ בָּרְכוּ אֱמוּנַי,
שָׂבַעְנוּ וְהוֹתַרְנוּ כִּדְבַר ה׳.

הַזָּן אֶת עוֹלָמוֹ רוֹעֵנוּ אָבִינוּ.
אָכַלְנוּ אֶת לַחְמוֹ וְיֵינוֹ שָׁתִינוּ.

עַל־כֵּן נוֹדֶה לִשְׁמוֹ וּנְהַלְּלוֹ בְּפִינוּ.
אָמַרְנוּ וְעָנִינוּ אֵין קָדוֹשׁ כַּה׳.

Let us bless the Rock from Whose bounty we have eaten. Our Shepherd and Father nourishes His universe; we have eaten His bread and drunk His wine–therefore let us thank Him and proclaim: "There is none as holy as God!"

YOM SHABBATON

Z'mirot Liturgy
Folksong

Yom Shabaton ën lish-ko-ach
Zichro k'rë-ach ha-ni-cho-ach
Yona matza vo ma-no-ach
V'sham ya-nu-chu y'gi-ë cho-ach

Hayom nichbad liv-në e-mu-nim
Z'hirim l'sham-ro avot u-va-nim
Cha-kuk bish-në lu-chot a-vanim
Më-rov o-nim v'amëtz ko-ach
Yo-na ma-tza vo ma-no-ach
V'sham ya-nu-chu y'gi-ë cho-ach

יוֹם שַׁבָּתוֹן אֵין לִשְׁכֹּחַ,
זִכְרוֹ כְּרֵיחַ הַנִּיחֹחַ,
יוֹנָה מָצְאָה בוֹ מָנוֹחַ,
וְשָׁם יָנוּחוּ יְגִיעֵי כֹחַ.

הַיּוֹם נִכְבָּד לִבְנֵי אֱמוּנִים,
זְהִירִים לְשָׁמְרוֹ אָבוֹת וּבָנִים,
חָקוּק בִּשְׁנֵי לֻחוֹת אֲבָנִים,
מֵרֹב אוֹנִים וְאַמִּיץ כֹּחַ.

פִּזְמוֹן:
יוֹנָה מָצְאָה בוֹ מָנוֹחַ,
וְשָׁם יָנוּחוּ יְגִיעֵי כֹחַ.

The Day of Rest must not be forgotten. Its memory is like a fragrant odor. It provides for the exhausted and it is honored by the faithful who carefully safeguard it.

HAVDALA

Allegro moderato

Liturgy
Folksong

הִנֵּה אֵל יְשׁוּעָתִי אֶבְטַח וְלֹא אֶפְחָד
כִּי עָזִּי וְזִמְרָת יָהּ הַשֵּׁם
וַיְהִי לִי לִישׁוּעָה.

Hi-në Ël y'shu-a-ti evtach v'lo efchad
Ki a-zi v'zimrat ya A-do-nai
Vay'hi li li-shu-a

Behold, God is my deliverance; I will trust, and will not be afraid; truly the Lord is my strength and my song; He has delivered me indeed.

AMAR RABI AKIVA

Moderato

Folksong

Amar Ra-bi Akiva:
V'ahav-ta l'rë-a-cha ka-mo-cha,
Ze klal gadol ba-to-ra

אָמַר רַבִּי עֲקִיבָא:
וְאָהַבְתָּ לְרֵעֲךָ כָּמוֹךָ,
זֶה כְּלָל גָּדוֹל בַּתּוֹרָה.

Thus saith Rabbi Akiba: "Thou shalt love thy neighbor as thyself. This is a major tenet of the Torah."

AMAR RABI ELAZAR

Liturgy
Folksong

Amar Ra-bi Elazar
Amar Ra-bi Chanina:
Tal-mi-dë cha-cha-mim mar-bim
Shalom ba-o-lam

אָמַר רַבִּי אֶלְעָזָר
אָמַר רַבִּי חֲנִינָא:
"תַּלְמִידֵי חֲכָמִים מַרְבִּים
שָׁלוֹם בָּעוֹלָם."

Rabbi Elazar said in the name of Rabbi Hanina, "The disciples of the sages increase peace throughout the world.

AVINU MALKENU

Liturgy
Folksong

אָבִינוּ מַלְכֵּנוּ חָנֵּנוּ וַעֲנֵנוּ
כִּי אֵין בָּנוּ מַעֲשִׂים
עֲשֵׂה עִמָּנוּ צְדָקָה וָחֶסֶד
וְהוֹשִׁיעֵנוּ.

Avinu malkënu cha-nënu va-a-nënu
Ki ën banu ma-a-sim
A-së imanu tz'daka va-chesed
V'ho-shi-ënu

Our Father, our King, be gracious unto us and answer us, for lo we are unworthy; deal with us in charity and lovingkindness and save us.

SIM SHALOM

שִׂים שָׁלוֹם טוֹבָה וּבְרָכָה.

Sim shalom to-va uv-ra-cha

O grant peace, happiness and blessing.

V'SAMACHTA B'CHAGECHA

Round
With spirit

Liturgy
Folksong

1

V' - sa - mach- ta b' - cha - ge - cha v' - ha - yi - ta ach sa - më-ach

ach ach sa - më - ach 1. ach 2. ach

2

v' - sa - mach - ta b' - cha - ge - cha v' - ha - yi - ta

ach sa - më - ach ach ach sa - më - 1. ach 2. ach

V'samachta b'cha-ge-cha
V'ha-yi-ta ach sa-më-ach

וְשָׂמַחְתָּ בְּחַגֶּיךָ וְהָיִיתָ אַךְ שָׂמֵחַ.

"And thou shalt rejoice in thy festivals and be glad."

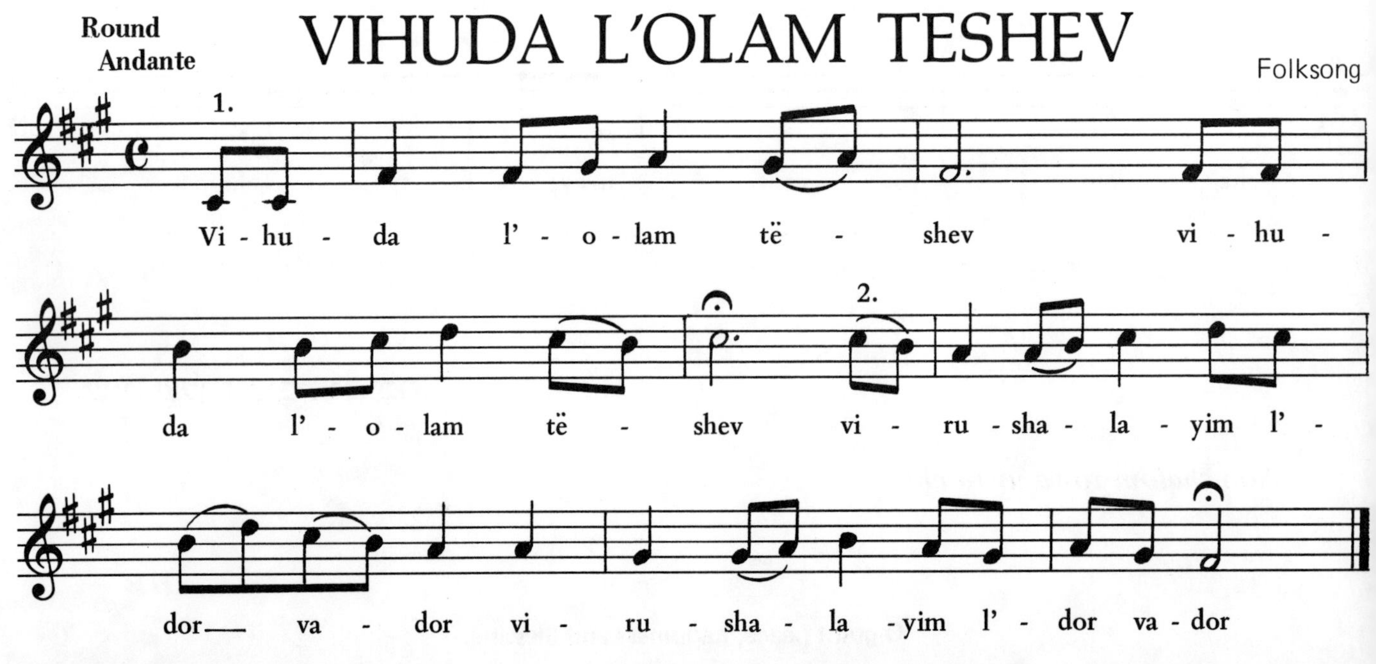

Vi-hu-da l'olam të-shëv
Vi-ru-sha-la-yim l'dor vador

וִיהוּדָה לְעוֹלָם תֵּשֵׁב וִירוּשָׁלַיִם לְדוֹר וָדוֹר.

The Jewish nation and Jerusalem are eternal

MI Y'MALEL

מִי יְמַלֵּל גְּבוּרוֹת יִשְׂרָאֵל אוֹתָן מִי יִמְנֶה
הֵן בְּכָל דּוֹר יָקוּם הַגִּבּוֹר גּוֹאֵל הָעָם
שְׁמַע! בַּיָּמִים הָהֵם בַּזְּמַן הַזֶּה
מַכַּבִּי מוֹשִׁיעַ וּפוֹדֶה —
וּבְיָמֵינוּ כָּל עַם יִשְׂרָאֵל יִתְאַחֵד יָקוּם וְיִגָּאֵל.

Mi y'malël gvu-rot Yisraël o-tan mi yim-ne
Hën b'chol dor ya-kum ha-gi-bor go-ël ha-am
Shma! ba-ya-mim ha-hëm baz-man ha-ze
Ma-ka-bi mo-shi-a u-fo-de—
Uv-ya-më-nu kol am Yisraël
Yit-a-chëd ya-kum v'yi-ga-ël

SINGABLE ENGLISH
Who can retell the things that befell us
Who can count them?
In ev'ry age, a hero or sage
Arose to our aid.
Hark! In days of yore
In Israel's ancient land
Brave Macabeus led the faithful band
But now all Israel must as one arise
Redeem itself through deed and sacrifice

SHIR YAYIN

Round
Music: W. A. Mozart
1.
Kos ni - sa rë - im kos ya - yin hën ko - chë - nu rav a -
da - yin lich - vod yë - ni u - vat ë - ni ya - rik kol
2.
ish ko - so mi - yad hoy bat - la - nim al ma tach - lo - mu
al ma tësh- vu al ma ti - do - mu tu - ram al kol
kir - u b' - kol tu - ram al kol kir - u v' - kol kir - u v' -
3.
kol ma - du - a ze pit - om pi - chem na - dam ma - du - a
ze pit - om pi - chem na - dam kir - u kir - u
kir - u b' - në cha - mor sho - të o - lam la -

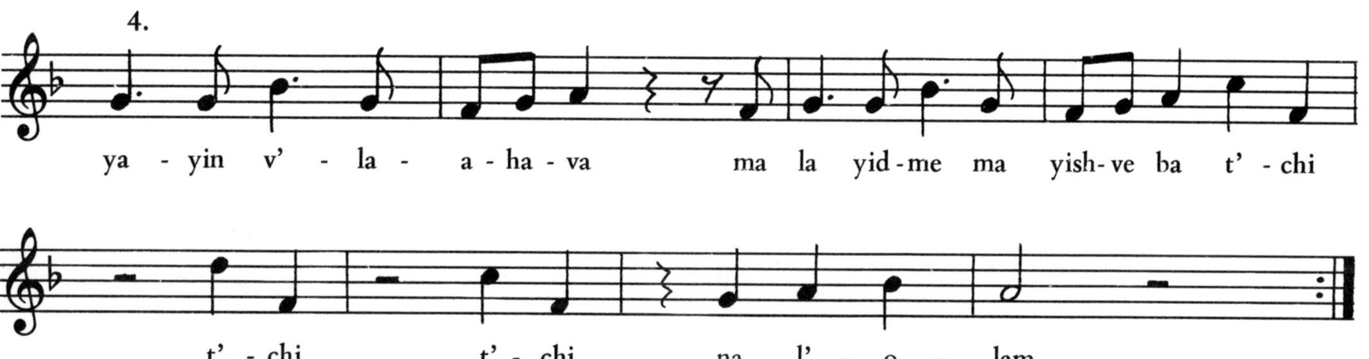

כּוֹס נִשָּׂא, רֵעִים, כּוֹס יַיִן.
הֵן כֹּחֵנוּ רַב עֲדַיִן.
לִכְבוֹד יֵינִי וּבַת עֵינִי
יָרִיק כָּל אִישׁ כּוֹסוֹ מִיָּד.
הוֹי, בַּטְלָנִים, עַל מַה תַּחְלֹמוּ?
עַל מַה תֵּשְׁבוּ, עַל מַה תִּדֹּמוּ?
תּוֹרַם עַל כֹּל, קִרְאוּ בְקוֹל!
מַדּוּעַ זֶה פִּתְאֹם פִּיכֶם נָדַם?
מַדּוּעַ זֶה פִּתְאֹם פִּיכֶם נָדַם?
קִרְאוּ, קִרְאוּ, קִרְאוּ
בְּנֵי חֲמוֹר. שׁוֹטֵי עוֹלָם!

לַיַּיִן וְלָאַהֲבָה!
מַה לָּהּ יִדְמֶה, מַה יִּשְׁוֶה בָּהּ?
תְּחִי, תְּחִי נָא לְעוֹלָם.

Kos nisa rë-im kos yayin
Hën kochënu rav ada-yin
Lich-vod yë-ni uvat ëni
Yarik kol ish koso mi-yad
Hoy, batlanim, al ma tach-lo-mu
Al ma tëshvu, al ma ti-do-mu
Turam al kol, kiru v'kol
Ma-du-a ze pitom pi-chem nadam
Ma-du-a ze pitom pi-chem nadam
Kiru, kiru, kiru
B'në cha-mor sho-të olam
La-ya-yin v'la-a-ha-va
Ma la yidme, ma yish-ve ba
T'chi, t'chi na l'o-lam

Come drink up — empty your cup. To the incomparable — wine and love. Live forever!

HI-NE MA TOV

Liturgy
Folksong

הִנֵּה מַה טּוֹב וּמַה נָּעִים
שֶׁבֶת אַחִים גַּם יָחַד.

Hi-në ma tov u-ma na-im
She-vet achim gam ya-chad

How good and pleasant it is for brothers to dwell together in unity.

HARMONIKA

Folksong

Hëy, har-mon-i-ka, nag-ni li,
She-yir-ad kol tzlil,
Et ha-ho-ra she-ra-kad-nu
ya-chad ba-ga-lil...

Ho-ra ho-ra
She-ra-kad-nu ya-chad ba-ga-lil!

Od niz-ko-ra
Et ha-ho-ra
She-ra-kad-nu ya-chad ba-ga-lil.

הֵי, הַרְמוֹנִיקָה, נַגְּנִי לִי,
שֶׁיִּרְעַד כָּל צְלִיל,
אֶת הַהוֹרָה שֶׁרָקַדְנוּ
יַחַד בַּגָּלִיל . . .

הוֹרָה הוֹרָה
שֶׁרָקַדְנוּ יַחַד בַּגָּלִיל!

עוֹד נִזְכֹּרָה
אֶת הַהוֹרָה
שֶׁרָקַדְנוּ יַחַד בַּגָּלִיל.

Accordion, play for us the Hora we danced long ago. We shall always remember the Hora which we danced in the Galilee.

HARO-A MIN HAGAI

Ka-a-sher të-a-tzam-na ë-nai
V'esh-kach et ed-ri v'yo-nai,
Od ez-kor, od ez-kor, y'di-dai,
Ha-ro-a hak-ta-na min ha-gai.

Ko-cha-vim yid-a-chu më-a-lai
V'ha-cho-shech y'chas et cha-yai
Ach a-ni od er-e l'fa-nai
Ha-ro-a hak-ta-na min ha-gai

כַּאֲשֶׁר תֵּעָצַמְנָה עֵינַי
וְאֶשְׁכַּח אֶת עֶדְרִי וְיוֹנַי,
עוֹד אֶזְכֹּר, עוֹד אֶזְכֹּר, יְדִידַי,
הָרוֹעָה הַקְּטַנָּה מִן הַגַּיְא.

כּוֹכָבִים יִדְעֲכוּ מֵעָלַי
וְהַחֹשֶׁךְ יְכַס אֶת חַיַּי,
אַךְ אֲנִי עוֹד אֶרְאֶה לְפָנַי
הָרוֹעָה הַקְּטַנָּה מִן הַגַּיְא.

When I close my eyes and forget my flocks
I will remember, my friends, the small shepherdess from the valley.

KI TINAM

Mi zot lik-ra-ti o-la
Bo-i a-cho-ti ka-la
Li-bav-ti-ni mi-ka-lot
Yaf-ya-fit li
Yaf-ya-fit li bam-cho-lot.

Ki ka-la ani, ki ani ka-la
Ki na-va a-ni kiv-not ha-a-ya-la
Bo-a v'na-chu-la, ki li-bi a-va
Ki tin-am ba-ma-chol a-ha-va

מִי זֹאת לִקְרָאתִי עוֹלָה
בֹּאִי אֲחוֹתִי כַּלָּה
לִבַּבְתִּנִי מִכַּלּוֹת
יָפְיָפִית לִי
יָפְיָפִית לִי בַּמְּחוֹלוֹת.

כִּי כַלָּה אֲנִי, כִּי אֲנִי כַלָּה
כִּי נָאוָה אֲנִי כִּבְנוֹת הָאֲיָלָה
בֹּאָה וְנָחוּלָה, כִּי לִבִּי אָבָה
כִּי תִנְעַם בַּמָּחוֹל אַהֲבָה.

O most beautiful of all brides, let us express
our love through the dance.

SHIBOLET BA-SA-DE

Shi-bo-let ba-sa-de
Ko-r'-a ba-ru-ach
Më-o-mes gar-i-nim ki rav
U-v'-mer-chav harim
Yom k'var ya-fu-ach,
Ha-she-mesh ke-tem v'za-hav

Uru, hoy, uru,
Shu-ru b'në kfar-im,
Ka-ma hën bash-la k'var
Al p'në ha-ka-rim.
Kitz-ru, shil-chu ma-gal,
Et rë-sheet ha-ka-tzir.

שִׁבֹּלֶת בַּשָּׂדֶה
כּוֹרְעָה בָּרוּחַ
מֵעֹמֶס גַּרְעִינִים כִּי רַב.
וּבְמֶרְחַב הָרִים
יוֹם כְּבָר יָפוּחַ,
הַשֶּׁמֶשׁ כֶּתֶם וְזָהָב.

עוּרוּ, הוֹי, עוּרוּ,
שׁוּרוּ בְּנֵי כְּפָרִים,
קָמָה הֵן בָּשְׁלָה כְּבָר
עַל פְּנֵי הַכָּרִים.
קִצְרוּ, שִׁלְחוּ מַגָּל,
עֵת רֵאשִׁית הַקָּצִיר.

Sheaf of wheat bending in the wind, the weight of grain so great,
And in the mountain range day is done, the sun is orange with gold.
Awake, O look, the wheat in the meadows is ripe.
Harvest, send sickle, the time of harvest has begun.

L'CHA DODI

Liturgy
M. Zeira

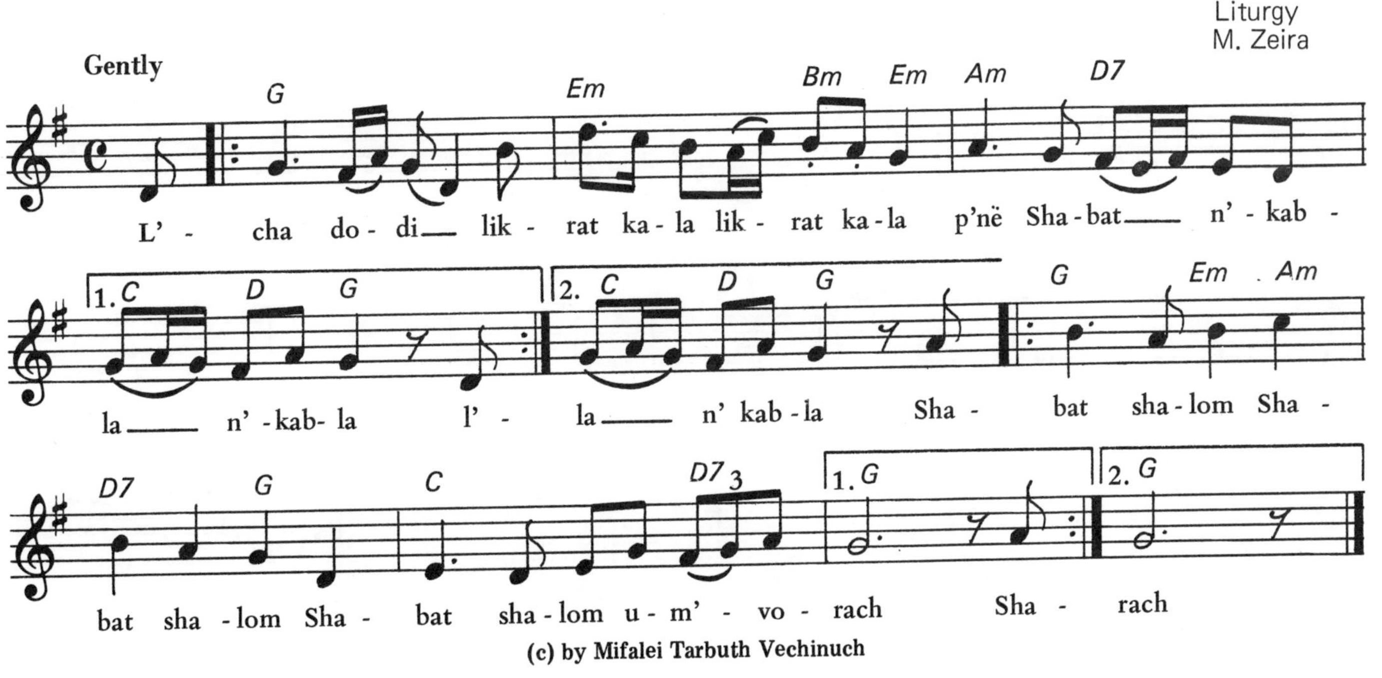

לְכָה דוֹדִי לִקְרַאת כַּלָּה,
פְּנֵי שַׁבָּת נְקַבְּלָה.
שַׁבָּת שָׁלוֹם וּמְבֹרָךְ

L'cha do-di lik-rat ka-la
P'në Sha-bat n'kab-la
Sha-bat shalom uv-ra-cha!

Come let us welcome in joy the Sabbath bride. A peaceful and blessed Sabbath.

SHER

SHERELE

DEBKA RAFIACH

DEBKA DALUNA

Lana Delray